MW00628656

Leathersex Q&A

Leathersex Q&A

Questions About Leathersex And The Leather Lifestyle Answered

Joseph W. Bean

Daedalus Publishing Company

Copyright © 1996 by Joseph W. Bean

All rights reserved. No part of this book may be reproduced or transmitted in any form or by any means, electronic or mechanical, including photocopying, recording or by any informational storage or retrieval system except with permission in writing from the publisher.

Published by Daedalus Publishing Company,
2140 Hyperion Avenue Los Angeles CA 90027 USA

Edited by Richard Labonte

Indexed by Victoria Baker

Cover design by Kari Svendsboe

Cover image by Heather B.

ISBN 1-881943-01-1

Library of Congress Catalog Card Number: 96-85421

Printed in the United States of America

Dedication

I dedicate this book to warren w. west.

What I learned from him about love and the magic of living in love will take a lifetime to make my own, and I will always be hoping to become able to teach someone else the same lessons. I also set this book as a milepost in my battle against his enemies (and scott's): prudery, homophobia, and AIDS.

About The Author

Joseph W. Bean has been involved in SM and leathersex for more than thirty years, and has written about gay and sexual issues for more than 20 years. He has written or created illustrations for dozens of gay and mainstream magazines, and edited more than a dozen. He is currently Managing Editor of *Bear*, *Powerplay*, *International Leatherman*, *RoundUp*, *Foreskin Quarterly*, *Bunkhouse*, and *Hombres Latinos*, the Brush Creek Media group of gay and erotic publications. His work appears in Mark Thompson's anthology *Leatherfolk* and Bill Warner's anthologies *Rogues of San Francisco* and *Country Rogues*, and he contributed to *Different Loving* (Brame et al), *The Encyclopedia of Unusual Sexual Practices* (Brenda Love), and *Safe Sane Consensual SM* (Roberts and West). He is the author of *Leathersex: A Guide for the Curious Outsider and the Serious Player*.

About the Author

Table of Contents

FOREWORD

I have known that *Leathersex Q&A* has been under construction for some time, and I have been very eager to get my hands on the manuscript. The fact is, I have been hoping for a book like this one to come along for quite a while now, because without it, there has been a large gap in the SM/leather/fetish literature. The book you are holding closes that gap in large measure, and for that, we can all be thankful.

For the last 15 years or so, there have been a relatively small number of us who have tried to write and speak about the leathersex experience in ways that would be useful to practitioners and others who are curious. I know that when we go "on the road" to teach in various cities, we almost always seem to generate more questions than we actually answer or even address in our presentations. These presentations almost always conclude with some question time for our audiences, but that rarely amounts to more than 30 minutes—if we are lucky enough to have even that much time. It is also true that many people are reluctant to ask us their questions "in public" for obvious reasons.

Additionally, those of us who have written books and published essays on various aspects of leathersex have the limitation of responding in our writing to the questions that we ourselves think are important to discuss. The existing books are not interactive; the standard book format just simply does not allow for it. This usually means that the material that writers and teachers have to offer is selected by us and not by you, our audience. Exceptions to this rule are rare, and in the SM literature all the more uncommon. We have had to guess about what will be important for you to hear or read and understand. Sometimes we have been good at that, and sometimes not.

Leathersex Q&A fixes this problem. At last we have a volume where the issues to be dealt with come from you, which is as it should be. No other book in the existing literature has been as reader-based as this one. And frankly, it is my opinion that no other person is as well-qualified to offer this solution as Joseph Bean.

There are three reasons I think this is so: First, in his positions as editor at *Drummer* magazine and later as Managing Editor at Brush Creek Media, publishers of *International Leatherman* and *Powerplay* (among others), Joseph has been uniquely positioned to have the leathersex audience write to him with questions that really matter. Second, Joseph Bean knows his subject and very well. He has been a devotee of leathersex since his teenage years—from Top to bottom, Master to slave, fetishist to exhibitionist, voyeur to dispassionate observer. And third, it is my belief that Joseph brings to his answers a rare combination of gifts: long experience, an uncompromising morality, a sharp intellect, formal spiritual training, a steady compassion, and a high regard for lust.

Throughout all Joseph's careful answers to carefully selected questions, his caring for the question's author, indeed, for all the people in the leathersex experience, is informed by his profound respect for humans, for our condition, for our frailty, for our sincerity, for our ignorance, and for our fears. Always, it is clear that Joseph is a person who is here to help. When he has biases, they are labeled such, so that we may choose for ourselves.

Foreword

Perhaps best of all, his approach is clear, direct, gentle—even loving. I feel safe with his ideas. As I read along, I know I am with a great teacher who is humbled by his own ignorance and the pains of his own learning. I am reassured that he will not condescend to me or mislead me. As I read along, I trust this man.

Joseph Bean is one of our living village elders. All too often, the elders in most kinds of villages eventually come to mix up their wisdom with equal parts of hidebound dogma and arrogance which forces listeners to sort these out from each other. In this book, Joseph avoids such mixing.

This will be enjoyable reading for both leathersex beginners and veterans partly because the writing is so personal, and partly because Joseph respects the questions so much. I have treasured the fact that Joseph and I are close friends. When I need fresh viewpoints about aspects of the leathersex experience, I know I can rely on him to offer new ideas in a way I can understand. He does the same thing for you in this book. Whether you agree with his answers to the deeply personal questions he responds to here or not, you will come away with new information and/or a new perspective. Joseph's first book, *Leathersex*, remains an important contribution to our literature; with the arrival of *Leathersex Q&A*, the work is complete in the sense that the interactive component has now been supplied. Together, they are a tour de force and essential reading for the leather/SM community.

Leatherville is a luckier place for having Joseph Bean in it. Whether one lives in the center of this amazing little town or way out in the suburbs, we can all be glad that Mr. Bean's particular appetites have led him to dwell among us. Quite simply, the reason is that his citizenship here, coupled with his numerous gifts and steady generosity, means that we get to share in the bounty of his fertile mind.

Guy Baldwin
Los Angeles, June 1996

PREFACE

The following letter arrived in the summer of 1994. Because it reached me just days after my slave warren died, it was set aside. In the ensuing shuffle, it was forgotten for several months. After checking with Barry, its writer, I decided to publish it as an example of the letters that provided the questions answered in this book, and to answer it with a copy of *Leathersex: A Guide for the Curious Outsider and the Serious Player*.

Dear Mr. Bean,

I've wanted to write to you on several occasions, but have basically "chickened-out" prior to today. I hope this correspondence does find its way to you and that you are able to accept it in the spirit I am striving to write it. I am certain to flatter you, but it is not my desire to intrude or necessarily "come on" to you. Should I overstep any boundaries, please attribute that to various hormonal imbalances on the part of a well-meaning "fan."

For a number of years now, I have picked up *Drummer* and other leather-oriented publications and made some new and sometimes frightening discoveries about myself. First of all, yes, leather and what I perceive to be a "leather lifestyle" turns me on. And, while I used to live in San Francisco and have visited a number of "leather" bars, the best I've been able to do are leather jackets. I can't seem to quite take "the plunge" or meet up with those I'd feel comfortable exploring several new territories with. I am also old enough to know by now that bars are not necessarily a great place to build good "friendships" or find "Mr. Right. . . ."

For me, the themes of honesty, sincerity, communication, trust and sensitivity are re-occurring and unavoidable.

Now, let me complicate this with what I think I've discovered about myself. I think I am a boy. I am certain I have no desire to be a "slave," although I am mostly submissive and enjoy being told what feels good/what to do, etc. I'm pretty sure, at this point, that "slave" and "boy" are not the same things, but I don't know how to find out what is truly comfortable for me.

I am not virginal, I've had two significant relationships and, I'll even confess to you, I'm already 40 years old. I am sexually a bottom, who can be versatile, but prefer being dominated, instructed, cared for and cared about. Light S/M and B/D excite me to a degree, but I have no desire for wounds and bruises or excessive pain. I've been called "boy" in bed by one of my previous lovers and I liked it. I also know that I am generally attracted to older, more experienced men.

Eventually, I suppose I'd like a terrific relationship with a man who understands this stuff, whose needs and interests are compatible with my own. While I seem to sometimes crave hot sex and nurturing, I am also a very nurturing man myself and have a lot to give. I want to, yes, look up to someone, but also be respected. I'd like to receive guidance and even be dominated in the bedroom, but I don't want to spend my life on my hands and knees outside safe and sane sexual situations. I am gaining or aspiring to activist status as a gay man, I am a professional person, a romantic, and a spiritual seeker; and I don't want to be abused or commanded to give up what I've achieved to date.

I know from experience that I do not wear a crew-cut very well and would hate being told to get one! (I'm striving for a little humor here, too.)

On the other hand, I think I crave training and a little instruction. And, I seem to have about three billion "TopDad/Boy" and leather fantasies. . . .

I recently started talking about this with a few trusted friends. Oh, my God, you wouldn't believe some of the reactions! I've heard "Go for it," and "Are you nuts?," various examinations of what "the leather scene" is all about, and several have blamed my ex-lover (who was abusive) for my now "liking abuse. . . ."

You, Mr. Bean, and I know I'm after something else, but don't really know how or where to begin. That's why I'm writing to you. Got any ideas?

I've seen a number of photos of you in the past and, yes, I find you very attractive. I am, however, looking to you as a respected member of the leather community, someone who might have been able to read between the lines here and hear, maybe, some of what I don't have the vocabulary to articulate as of yet. I would be very flattered if you could take the time to share of your thoughts or suggestions with me. If you can or want to respond, feel free to contact me however it is most appropriate for you.

I'm hoping to visit San Francisco several times during the summer. While I mention this because I think you live in the Bay Area and would love to meet you, I also state it because I'm concerned that should I try to act on these desires/fantasies that I do so with good information. I think SF might present more opportunities for . . . whatever . . . than what I'm used to dealing with.

Incidentally, a while back, I was approached in a local establishment by a very hot, fully leather-clad man, who I thought was going to "come on" to me. Honestly, my knees turned to jell-o and I know I blushed. What happened instead floored me! He proposed that I model leather for him and his lover's custom leather business in brochures, etc. I explained that I didn't really have any leather. He proposed that I do the modeling in exchange for the leather. "Great," I thought. . . . Well, I'm still "waiting" for the call. But I mention this because it really seemed to reveal to me that maybe what I feel inside isn't crazy and maybe the "time has come. . . ." Obviously, someone else momentarily saw through the yuppie garb and layer of "bar protection" I usually wear. . . .

Anyway, Mr. Bean, thank you for your time and, I hope, a kind receiving of this letter. I'd love to hear from you and of any suggestions you might have with regard to my "situation," whenever it might be convenient.

If I have offended or stepped on anyone else's toes, please again consider this "fan mail" and no more or less.

Be well and thanks again! If you do call, the people I live with are cool, and it's fine to leave specific info on the machine, should you get the machine and not me.—Barry

I suppose I will never know why leathermen started sending such letters to me. In 1987, when the first of my leathersex columns began to be published in gay newspapers, some of the papers ran an invitation for readers to send in questions, but there were never many letters resulting directly from the column, and none of the papers chose to run the few Q and A pieces I offered. When I wrote editorials in *Drummer*, I often invited readers to respond with questions, suggestions, or opinions of their own, but the response per editorial usually ran about zero or one. And when I appeared regularly on Electric City Cheap TV as the Leathersex Faerie, I answered questions and invited further queries, but most of the questions I answered on the air came from my files. Those old files full of letters asking about leathersex and the leather lifestyles had started to accumulate in the early 1980s, long before I first publicly said I'd answer them. Today, having intentionally made myself available to answer questions, the influx has slowed from a 1985 high of about 65-70 letters to the current rate of about 10 in the past 12 months.

Over the years I have responded directly to about three-quarters of the letters. I chose not to answer written questions from friends, feeling that the dynamics of friendship would be threatened by the resulting teacher/seeker tone. I never answered letters in which I felt I was being dared or challenged to respond "correctly." And I didn't answer questions I thought were genuinely and rightly answered only by professionals in medicine, law, or religion.

Now, I think, I have a new reason not to answer some of my mail. I can say, as I now do to Barry, that I have answered the questions posed in either *Leathersex* or *Leathersex Q&A*, and offer to answer questions individually only if the writer has already read both books. Well, I probably won't be able to stick to that, but it feels good to think I might.

This book is made up almost entirely of the questions I have answered by mail in the past 10 to 12 years. Unfortunately for me, although I filed the questions, I never kept copies of my answers. So, these are 1994-95 responses to questions posed from 1983 to 1994. In several cases, as many as 10 similar questions have been stitched together to form a single query for this manuscript. In a few cases, complex questions have been broken into smaller components to make both the question and the answer more accessible here.

A small number of the questions in this book were proposed by warren and our friend Bear-Dog who, after reading the original question list, thought the additions would be useful.

Obviously, this book owes the very possibility of its existence to the men who asked the questions. I have become a better and more thoroughly informed person through the thinking, research, and conversations that have led to the answers. I owe the writers of the questions an inestimable debt which my letters and this book barely begin to repay.

I also recognize my great indebtedness to Victoria Baker and Don Bersticker, who volunteered to read this book in its roughest form and to contribute to it by pointing out my errors and suggesting improvements. Without their help I know I'd never have reached the point of liking this manuscript enough to let you read it.

Finally, I owe more than I can say to warren w. west who was my slave, lover, and best friend through most of the writing of the book. He laughed when I got silly, then respectfully pointed me back in the direction we both wanted the book to go. He stayed up nights to read and comment on the manuscript, and got up early to make my breakfast and see me off to work. He kept my house and my life in order, filled my playroom with delightful noises, warmed my bed, and made sense of my jumbled existence. Warren died with AIDS in July, 1994. My life and this book would be better if he had lived.

To the friends who have remained friends while I have ignored them for the sake of this book, I can only say that I appreciate their patience and look forward to returning their kindness more fully after the book gets strong enough to move out of Daddy's house and make a life for itself.

Joseph W. Bean
San Francisco, March 1995

1

QUESTIONS FROM NOVICES

A lot of the questions I get in the mail are from novices, people who are new to leathersex, often with no experience at all. Their questions frequently include lengthy descriptions of the pain they experience coming out as gay and as leathermen. Because they are usually unable to frame a simple question that will encompass the swirling emotions and confusing impressions they are living with, I am often drawn to write lengthy responses, allowing myself to stray far from the questions actually posed. In this chapter, I have attempted to retain some sense of the confusion and emotionality of newcomers to leathersex, while eliminating the long turns and circuitous verbiage of the original questions and answers.

I'm new to doing SM, even though I've been reading and fantasizing for years. My problem is that everyone is being too gentle with me, treating me like the "baby" I would be without

all those years of books and dreams. Does this initiation period end soon? How do I speed the process?

I have to guess that the overly gentle treatment you are eager to end has to do with the way you are handled in scenes involving pain. If so, your first and best option is to speak to your Tops about your limits before the scene. Don't lie. Don't guess that you are limitless or suggest that you might be. Tell them what you have told me, that you are not getting the level of stimulation you believe you could handle and enjoy. Frankly, Tops often wish their bottoms could handle more than they can. Being Tops, they enjoy doling out the stimulation—pain, if you will—and are usually more satisfied themselves if they are able to do a lot of it, and fairly intensely. This is, of course, not true of all Tops, particularly novice Tops. All Tops have limits, just as bottoms do. They reach a point where they become uncomfortable, for whatever reason, and do not want the scene to intensify any further. Maybe, at least at times, you are playing with Tops whose limits are less advanced than your own. Even though you are new to the scene, this is entirely possible.

If you have trouble talking to Tops about this sort of thing, your next step in becoming a safe and satisfied SM player is to learn to talk about your desires. Until you can do this, you are unlikely to get the scenes you want, and very likely to get into scenes you don't want, ones that may disappoint you in ways other than being too gentle.

Talking before the scene, which is generally called negotiating the scene, is only the first device available to you for getting more of the kind of working over you want. In negotiation—however formal or ritualized or casual it may actually be, depending on the conditions of the moment—it is your job to see that the person you may be about to play with knows what you are hoping to experience and how much of it you believe you can bear, what you hope will be avoided and whether he is free to experiment somewhat with your distaste. You don't have to lie to let a Top know that you do not wish to be treated as a novice. So, don't say you're an old hand, but do say you are more concerned about being treated too gently than too roughly.

The other very useful method available to you should not be seen as an alternative. Rather, it is the companion of negotiation. Observe yourself as you play, giving special attention to the ways in which you react to the pain you are given. And, no less important, observe how the Top responds to your reactions. You may discover that you are telling the Top—either with body language or your voice—that you are reaching your limit even though you are not. If you groan as though you are truly being hurt, a good Top who is not familiar with your scene behavior will probably pull back and even begin to wind down the scene. If you pull away from the strokes, tense before the blows, or wince as the pain is administered, you are again likely to be understood as saying something like, "hold back a bit, I am not handling this level of stimulation well."

Granted, some bottoms feel they "need" to react in these ways, or find they can't avoid such reactions. If that is the case for you, you have to return to method one: negotiation. Tell the Top that you will "overreact" and that you may resist, but that you want some other way of slowing or stopping the scene, and you want your "overreactions" to be ignored. The new method of communicating you will be asking for is called a safeword. If a Top doesn't want to give you at least one safeword when you feel you need it, think seriously about whether you might want to look for another Top.

A safeword is a sound (or even an action) that you will use to communicate a specific message to the Top. Most people use safewords to communicate only "negative" messages such as slow down and stop, but you might need one specifically to say, "Give me more." Or, you might be allowed, if it doesn't damage the mood for your Top, to communicate directly by saying "More!"

when that is exactly what you mean.

Since I started going to SM parties, I keep hearing SM lyrics in pop music. Is this real, or am I just reading it into the music I like? Don't people notice this?

I suspect the most correct answer to your question falls under the infamous heading: E) All of the Above. SM lyrics do show up in pop music like the "some people want to abuse you/some people want to be abused" in "Sweet Dreams" (Eurhythmics), but they are seldom absolutely and unequivocally SM lyrics. For instance, businessmen might hear a description of deal-making in the quoted lines, and mental health professionals might hear the extremes of one scale of styles people have for interacting with one another.

If an artist like Madonna supplies confirming visuals in a music video, movie, or photo book, you may guess that your sexual take on the words is definite. Or, more precisely, that the artist accepts that as *one* reasonable interpretation of the song. Art, however, is art, and the best of it finds resonance in a wide range of human experience. Often, the artists may be unaware of the SM interpretations derived from their lyrics, which is not to say they'd be shocked or displeased to have you hear the song your way (especially if you paid retail for it).

A few songs that have done well in the pop markets (rock, punk, techno, etc.) have seemed to me very intentionally SM-related, but I know I'd hear of other ways to understand the songs if I started listing their titles. What's more, I get more pleasure from the slight twisting it takes to hear my life reflected in lyrics that are probably not meant to have such meaning.

As for what others hear, who knows? People like Tipper Gore (before the 1992 presidential campaign, of course) made a big deal of hearing sexual messages in just about all pop music. On the other hand, who would dispute that the music of teens and young adults has been largely about sex for as long as there has been music. It seems that some people, bent on censorship for whatever goals, hear representations of sex, promiscuity, homosexuality, and sadomasochism everywhere. That's understandable too. Once you proclaim yourself a dragonslayer, you must turn up dragons enough to keep yourself employed.

Want a more direct answer to your question? Okay. There have to be kinky song writers writing kinky lyrics in every possible level of disguise and evidence. Sometimes we notice.

How do I say no and get away when I meet a creep (or less than a god, anyway) through a personal ad or BBS?

"Thank you for your interest, but this is just not going to work for me," will do nicely. Of course, you will want to have kept that option open to yourself. If you've made a date that begins with you being bound and possibly gagged before you have a chance to discover he's a creep, things can become pretty difficult. If it is hard to escape and run away, or even to say "Yes, Sir, thank you, Sir," think how much harder it will be to say a believable "No."

The next question and answer may be of interest to you as well.

I'm "chatting" with a BBS Top who wants to beat me bloody, and he makes it sound so hot, but how do I check out a guy based only on his BBS "handle"?

Only a few days ago my friend Piglet called. He'd been chatting with a Top on a BBS and had set a play date. Before setting a definite date, he reeled off the names of people he thought the Top might know in the city where the Top lived, and listened as the Top reacted to the names. As it happens, I was one of the people Piglet mentioned and BBS Top said he knew me. Within 24 hours, I got a call from Piglet, who was checking the Top's reputation as I perceived it. Next day, the Top's lover dropped by my office and casually mentioned Piglet, following up the mention with a few pertinent questions.

Use your network regardless of where you meet a potential partner. Do not make anonymous dates on the basis of enticing promises and BBS handles. That is, don't make such dates without understanding you are risking a great deal when you do.

I'd say that if you want to reduce the risk and can't do so by using a network of leathersex friends, set up a public date before agreeing on a private play time. Even an hour or two together at a bar would be of some help before you meet a stranger in the dark privacy of his dungeon.

Most of my friends are gay, as I am, but they are not into leather or SM. They make jokes and derisive remarks about leathermen, and I never know what to say or do. It makes me feel personally attacked, and helpless.

You say you feel that the jokes and derisive remarks are personal attacks. Anyone who tries to tell you that these remarks should not be taken as personal attacks is defending the skeletons in his own closet and, by ignoring his own pain or discomfort, may be risking his own psychological health in the process. In fact, any derisive remark about any human beings—even if you are not a member of the class, type or group being demeaned—is a personal attack to a sensitive and well-meaning person.

Let me tell you where I learned this important lesson: When I was 20, and *The Advocate* was just getting started, I somehow happened to be helping then-publisher Dick Michaels at the office. I believe I was setting headline type at the time. Jim Kepner, then a reporter for *The Advocate*, came in and, while he was waiting to talk to Dick, he asked me what was the matter. He had come to the conclusion that something was bothering me just by looking at me. (That's the kind of perceptive genius Mr. Kepner is!) I told him that even though no one said such things about me, it was bothering me that I never spoke up when the people at my regular job in a bank data center told fag jokes or tried to insult each other by calling one another "queer" or "faggot."

He didn't miss a beat. "Tell the people who say such things that you are offended by jokes and other remarks at *anyone's* expense."

It seemed to me that I had nothing but my discomfort to lose. If my remarks made others guess that I was gay, I figured I could live with that. The shift supervisor at the data center was a very hot man who kept my dick jumping until I began hearing his fag jokes. That very night, I piped up when he made the first derogatory remark about "sissies." I told him I felt that any attack on anyone was inappropriate and made me uncomfortable. "You never know," I added impromptu, "who may be overhearing you."

"Why," he drawled, "you're no faggot."

"What makes you think *that*?" I asked.

"Oh, god, I didn't mean to hurt you, Buddy," he said in a voice and tone that made me believe he meant it sincerely.

Not half an hour later I heard my supervisor make some kind of wise-crack about women—women drivers, I think it was—and I repeated my original comment about appropriateness and my comfort.

"Now, I *know* you're not a woman . . . ," he started. Then, in a flash, he got it. "I see," he said, "it's *not* just about you, then, is it? Nah. . . ." And he went away, shaking his head. About two weeks later, when people were beginning to ask why our supervisor wasn't telling offensive jokes any more, there was a departmental meeting. We were told that racial jokes, "including jokes about such races as Mormons and homosexuals," would no longer be tolerated. The reference to Mormons was added, as I understood right away, to shift some of the weight of the situation off of those of us who worked together every night, and onto the vice president in charge of the data center, known to be a Mormon and sensitive to anti-religious statements and profanity.

I keep feeling romantic even though I wear leathers. I mean, I still think of flowers and chocolates as love gifts. I want to say "I love you" to men who've beaten me black and blue. Am I sick?

No, boy, you're not sick at all—not in any negative way—unless you count love-sick. I am a pretty seasoned Top and, although I cannot answer for other Tops, I can tell you that I enjoy romantic gifts and cuddly moods. Couldn't live without them. Nonetheless, a warning may be in order: Don't jump to the conclusion that a specific Top will take kindly to your Valentine moods and actions, but test the waters with *after-the-scene* presents. I can't imagine a Top who wouldn't like to get flowers or something of the sort then. (Even flowers can be "butched up" as required.) If nothing else, it settles any doubts—usually unspoken, of course—about his performance. You wouldn't be giving him a present if you were offended, disappointed, unsatisfied, or whatever.

How important is all the signaling by right and left colored hankies, keys, collars, etc.? I don't get it, and I'm not sure I want to bother.

I would feel very foolish using the word important to describe the traditional Top/bottom and preferred-activity signaling you mention. What is important unfolds between two people after they have made some kind of initial contact. The signaling devices are useful shorthand to help people figure out with whom they would be glad to make contact. Until and unless you begin to feel the need for them, don't bother with the hankies and such, although you are likely to find that the simple matter of wearing your keys, boot strap, wallet chain or something right or left is, after all, worthwhile. The basic question of whether a guy is planning to be Top (wearing signals on the left) or bottom (on the right) is one that others around him in the bar might reasonably like to have answered without clumsiness. Still, nothing is required or even important, just very possibly useful.

I've responded to at least 20 personal ads in *Drummer*, but I got answers from only four guys. I don't live in a big metropolis, so I need to make "anonymous" contacts, but none of the four I heard from were anything like the he-men in their ads. How can a guy in "anytown, USA" get by in leathersex?

It seems to me that you are asking several questions, but I will focus not on the vagaries of personal ads (not just now, anyway), but your stated question.

I have come to believe that there are kinky people, ready willing and able to play, everywhere. Finding them is the problem. And, in less-than-metropolitan settings, finding them is actually only step one. You then have to sort out the psychos from the cops from the fantasists from the real, live players. (Since I happen to know you live less than three hours drive from Washington, DC) I can suggest that you spend a few weekends in big city bars or at major events, making your perplexity about finding folks who live nearer your home a primary topic of conversation. It may cut down on your actual erotic contacts for the weekend (or not), but it will soon yield the harvest you want. Even if you discover that no one knows of players who live *that* near your home, you will turn up people who are willing to travel that far to be with you, and/or people who happen to travel through your area often, and/or people who know someone who knows the people in your area. Or, at the very least, you will find yourself talking to people, and probably developing friendships or other relationships worth frequent trips to the city. This is not your only option, but if the personals aren't working, it is a good one.

Other methods that have worked for other guys include telephone "sex" lines which are useful for much more than phone sex if you choose the right ones, hopping into the appropriate discussions and getting onto the right mailing lists on the Internet (by computer), and using the bulletin boards of bars and bookstores as near to or far from your home as you happen to go.

Is SM a team effort, or is the bottom supposed to be allowed to "sit back and leave the driving to" me?

Yes and yes. In my experience, the best leathersex does come about by a team effort with the bottom not just communicating but also participating in various ways. If nothing else, the bottom needs to kick into action on command for certain types of scenes. I mean, where would body worship or boot licking go with a too-passive bottom. But even in pain scenes—flogging, for instance—I always want the bottom's attention to be on helping me make the most of it for as long as he is in control of his attention. Many bottoms, perhaps all under the right conditions, lose control of their attention at extreme levels of play. They may call it "going away" or "slipping out," or describe it as "becoming involuntary" or in some other way, but a good Top will recognize this condition, and cease to expect attentive feedback from the bottom who enters it. Now, there are no rules, and I do know a few Tops who really want their partners to be little more than rag dolls once the scene gets rolling. I'd say that I don't approve of such scenes, except that I have watched them and seen that they work very well for the right people at the right time. What's more, I have heard bottoms praising the very Tops I mentioned, saying they felt relieved of responsibility, able to "get into it" faster, and so forth. Everything is possible, and everything does happen.

If I lick boots, sniff socks, and suck toes, does it mean I'm into SM? The only men who aren't freaked out by my fetish seem to be leathermen, but I don't like much of the rest of what they want me to do or let them do.

SM, in my opinion, is defined by the players. If you want to get at a guy's feet, but also want to say you are not into SM, do that. Just don't expect to be understood clearly without giving a more detailed statement. It's true that leathermen, generally, are more open to fetishes and other twists of sexuality than your garden variety homo-male, and it is true that leathermen are more comfortable talking about the "who will do what to whom" area of sexual expression. So, talk. I've been known to go to a party intent on using a full range of whips, only to spend the evening with a boy wrapped around my feet, licking and massaging, and hopping up from time to time to get me a drink or something. You could at least go that far couldn't you—just getting the man a drink or otherwise responding to his dominance—which is just an extra step toward the other guy's sexual ideal in exchange for getting what you want.

Are bars the only place to find leathermen? There have to be sober alternatives!

Alternatives to bars do exist. Genuinely sober alternatives may be harder to come up with in most places. Perhaps the good news for you is that the bars are not as drunk as they used to be, not by a long shot, and this means that the clean and sober energy is making headway in the leather meeting-place market. Usually club parties do permit drinking, but people do a lot less of it at such events than they do when they're out at the bars. Often the best social gatherings at major leather events are drinking affairs, but you'll be surrounded by more sobriety at the early evening events than the later ones, and at the host hotel events rather than the bar-sponsored ones. What's more, at most major leather events, there are 12-step meetings which would be a good place to start up the friendships which might lead to developing regular meetings or parties in or near your home for people who want to meet leathersex friends and partners without having to deal with booze.

Another series of options can be opened to you if you choose to wear your leathers or other leathersex identifying cues to the kinds of places you already like to go. Leatherfolk are everywhere, you know. If you went to a regular 12-step meeting wearing leathers, you'd get the attention of other leathermen, and you would have created opportunities for yourself. You might find the same kind of success wearing leather or whatever to your church, social clubs, the movies, or wherever. You have to be as careful as your own comfort demands, but there are bound to be some opportunities in your life if you have the courage to take advantage of them.

Are real leathermen on/in the scene 24 hours a day?

Your question leaves me wondering how you (or anyone) would go about defining either "real leathermen" or "in the scene." But, no matter the definitions, the answer is that many leathermen I would consider real are *not* in the scene 24 hours a day. Then, at the risk of revealing my own stodginess, I should add that once upon a time, I and the leathermen around me considered that we were in the scene *absolutely* 24 hours a day, seven days a week, but that was because we defined ourselves by a sharing of a specific ethical code and by complete submission (Tops and bottoms) to a sense of fraternity that we said we valued above all else. Maybe I grew up in a particularly strait-laced crowd, but I can tell you that being "in the scene" all the time in that sense was very comforting and well worth the constraints it put on me. Now, as the nature of the leather community has broadened, and as leathermen have diverged from one another by what they're into, what they speak of and believe in, etc., the concept behind the words "in the scene" has had to be narrowed in order to remain inclusive. Maybe what it comes down to is this: Almost no one except a contractual slave is in the scene all the time today in an obvious and intense way, but we are all in the scene all the time to varying degrees of intensity and involvement 24 hours of every day. *And*, it is only fair to say, the result is that your question may honestly be answered with either a yes or a no—choose the one you are comfortable with.

I can't afford fancy equipment like leather sleepsacks and custom straitjackets, but I like heavy, long-term bondage, and I enjoy being restrained in leather. What can I do without robbing a bank or two?

You can do everything without robbing banks, I promise. If you really want these things, you will scrimp and save as necessary to eventually own them, but they are not important. You could just as well be zipped into a sleepsack that is owned by someone else. In fact, it is not at all unusual for the Top to keep the bondage gear which is used on the bottom. Meantime, for about 15% of the cost of a sleepsack, you could buy a tanned hide. Being wrapped in that hide with snug ropes trussed over it might be as good as *or better than* being slipped and zipped into a sleepsack. What else? Leather for the body parts where it matters most is another option. If you want the leather on your hands, gloves or bondage mitts might help. If you mainly need the smell of the leather or the feel of it on your face, a hood or a bandanna-size swatch of leather might do the job. Use your imagination and call on the imagination of friends to get what you want, and remember that the expensive toys have almost all been developed as mass-market replacements for successful homemade toys. Get creative.

I worry about wearing my locked-on chain collar through airports and other metal detectors. Shouldn't I have a key so I can take it off for such times?

It is my opinion that a collar is a sign of submission which should not be removed by anyone but the man who put it on you.

That is an opinion rooted in old-school thinking, but one which I believe has enough inherent sense to remain true today. If not, why bother with the lock? If your problem with the metal detectors is nothing more than your embarrassment, learn to live with it. People think what they choose to think about one another. You having a locked-on neck chain will not cause the security guard at the airport to notice you all that much in a world where he is dealing with much stranger—not to mention more dangerous—things every day.

You might consider requesting a replacement for the chain collar, however. My last slave, warren, wondered if he could be allowed to remove his chain while going to visit his mother in Kansas for a week. My senses reeled. I didn't for a moment see the collar as the be-all and end-all of our relationship, but I couldn't imagine having a slave (especially one who would be out of the house) not wearing a collar. We considered putting a gold chain around his neck, one which a mother would take to be jewelry, and which she would not notice was "endless" and too small to slip over his head. Instead, we were able to get a collar tattooed around his neck, far enough down and out that he could cover it with a T-shirt. No lump, no noise, no problem.

It bothers me to break the rhythm of a scene to check in with a bottom, to be sure that I haven't overstepped his limits or left his restraints on too long. Is there any system to this that works better than a verbal check-in?

There are endless ways to check on the progress and safety of a scene within the confines of the power exchange. I'll give you a few ideas, but your own new ideas will be the ones that work best in the scenes you create.

My own preference is to remain completely, so to say, in character, but frankly admit what I am checking. Sometimes I even speak of what I am doing, but with words tailored to the scene. I might, for instance, say, “I'm planning to keep you strung up like this for a long time, so I want to hear about it if anything starts hurting when I'm not hitting it. Right now, I want to know about your hands. Are they getting cold or numb at all?” Then, regardless of the answer, I might add, “Let me just check for myself.” This method may take more thought and practice than most, particularly if you or your bottoms need to have a seamless mood created around the scene.

Another approach is the “harmless subterfuge” tactic. If it might be hands, again, that we want to check on: “Spread your hands out, no fists allowed!” Follow your words with a spreading of the fingers using your own hands to do it. If you discover any coldness, create a moment in which hesitation will deliver a message about numbness or cramping, and you don't break your stride. Besides, you banish fist-making, which is often a sign of tension being built up in a way that is likely to have detrimental effects on the scene.

One more: I like to create a rhythm of alternating intensity and tenderness. This makes it easy to move between heavy blows (for the majority of the time and experience) and light caresses (for rare moments and the *collecting of nonverbal feedback*). The lighter blows can even become slow, smoothing rubs of the open hand over the body parts you want to check, even if those parts are not otherwise involved in the scene at that moment.

If you are concerned about whether you have overstepped the bottom's limits, there are few ways of handling it better than having already put a safeword in place, policing the situation yourself by remaining open to *all* the feedback you get from the bottom, and allowing a break in the scene where necessary if you begin to distrust your reading of the bottom's body language and sounds.

I'm new to Topping and not all that experienced as a bottom. I've heard a lot about Tops reading the bottom's body lan-

guage, and I find myself unsure of what I am looking for and what it means. Is this something that can be explained in so many words or is it in the realm of experience being the only teacher?

The reading of body language is, as you guessed, largely developed from experience, both general leathersex experience for a general grammar of body language and specific experience of a particular bottom for a more detailed understanding of that person's body language. Nonetheless, some elements of body language are simple and nearly universal.

Let's think together about signs that might be invitations to continue and others that might be asking the Top to back off. A back that rolls gently, then spreads and rises slightly between flogging strokes seems to strongly invite more of the same attention. If the same back thrusts itself toward the strokes in sudden jerks, still spreading out the target area, I'd say the message is that the bottom wants not just more of the same, but harder or faster strokes. Conversely, if the back turns away or dips even one shoulder away from the strokes, I'd take it that the pain level is too high or rising too fast. Certainly, if a back caves in, shrinking the target area, I'd back off and think seriously about checking on what was wrong before continuing.

Similar message-bearing movements can be seen in other body parts. The butt and chest, for instance, can give signals effectively identical to the ones described for the back. Leg movements tend to emphasize turning and twisting, but are easily understood as offering the stroked area for further strokes, or attempting to move the affected area out of the line of fire.

Further into a scene—in terms of the bottom's psychology or limits rather than the time passed in the scene or its level of intensity—there are other types of signals given by the bottom's body. These are not body language in the usual sense of the word, meaning that they are not conscious or even semi-conscious, rather they are completely automatic responses to stimulation. Quivering muscles, rhythmic lurching of the entire body, and overall shivering fall into this category. The messages of these automatic responses are harder to generalize, but it is almost never true that the bottom wants to have the scene stopped because of them. To find out what the bottom is experiencing and get a reading as to whether he is hoping for you to continue despite his involuntary quivering, lurching and shivering, slow up a bit, touch the part of the body you are stimulating, and watch for the reaction to your touch. If there is no noticeable reaction, keep the action very slow or on hold until you are getting some reaction. When you get a reaction it will be at least semi-conscious, and probably easily understandable.

Obviously, there is a great deal more that could be said on this subject, but most of it can be learned better from experience than from a book. Besides, a Top sensitive enough to translate words from a book or class into action is also likely to be able to take the simple statements here as an adequate starting point for his practical study.

I've heard a lot about negotiating a scene, but I've never had the opportunity. Granted, I wouldn't know what to do if a man said, "Okay, now negotiate." What does it mean, and what should I do?

Negotiation is not always obvious, and it is very likely that you have been doing it all along. Doing it intentionally may be more effective, or not, depending on who you are and who your Tops may be. In the final analysis, negotiation is nothing more than working out an agreement with another person that includes what will, what might, and what must not be done; what intensity is surely, likely, probably not, and certainly not acceptable; and what general parameters each party considers essential or desirable. If, for example, you and the Top in question both know you are going to be doing a scene primarily made up of flogging and slapping, that you can take a great deal of these stimulations, and that you will stop him by using a safeword if something goes wrong, you have the basics covered.

Sometimes people want to know a great deal about a scene in advance, and to have some part in determining a lot of the details. You should find ways to express yourself to the Top on the questions that matter to you. The necessary statements might be made formally, in the language of the Top-bottom dynamic, in a mode that furthers the sense of the roles you and he are moving into. Alternatively, given the right atmosphere, a bottom can express a great deal in a casual way by mentioning a previous good or bad experience in some detail or by wondering aloud whether playing with the man at hand might lead to this or that experience he wishes to explore.

If it is necessary for you to stop just before the scene gets rolling and ask for time to negotiate, two rules might apply. First, at that point the word negotiate may feel threatening to a Top, appearing to convey a sense of apprehension on your part which could be bad for the confidence level he starts the scene with. So, call it talking, or telling him a few things he might find useful in controlling you, or whatever. Second, if you take such an opportunity to say things, you must see that you accommodate his need to do the same and that you speak of everything you feel you need to bring up.

What should or might be covered in negotiating a scene varies from person to person, and should be as little as is needed, giving the nature and flow of the scene and the nature and intentions of the Top as much room to operate freely as possible. But you may want to mention any of these things (or others): Consider the types of activities you want, don't want, and might like; the level of pain you believe you can process successfully; the acceptability or annoyance value of talking during the scene; your willingness to go along with verbalized fantasies, humiliation, and orders; any buzz words or activities you know are destructive of the appropriate leathersex attitude in yourself; and the place of your genitals and his in the scene. To clarify the question about genitals, you might ask whether your cock will be ignored and your orgasm with it, whether you will be permitted to come, and even to beat off while you are being used. And you might want to know if his cock is a reward you are to earn, a site you are expected to service, or not a player in the upcoming scene.

Definitely see that the person you are playing with knows of any physical limitations or medical conditions you have. Poor vision and contact lenses fall into this category along with arthritic joints, stuffy nasal passages, any tendency to faint or hyperventilate, and any recent or current medical treatments or drugs you may be taking. The general rule in disclosing anything to the Top, especially before a scene that might become intense for you, is that if it comes to mind it ought to be mentioned.

On the other hand, trying to discuss every possible point of interest or pushing for details better left to develop as they will can be destructive of scene mood, or place severe limits on what is possible in the scene. In other words, don't overnegotiate. Just be clear about what must be said, and be brief.

How can you put together a scary scene in a world where bottoms expect to negotiate a scene before it begins?

This is simple: Negotiate the needs and limitations of the bottom, even interrogate him thoroughly to be sure that your scary scene is not going to violate his limits in any significant way. Determine whether the bottom has medical limitations, for instance, that you must take into consideration. This questioning (which is really just negotiation carried on in a more than usually formal way) might even be a scene in itself, allowing you to collect a great deal of information that will be useful for developing a deeply frightening scenario. Then set a date for the actual scene, knowing that you can now keep the remaining negotiations very simple. In fact, the negotiating at the time of the scene will probably be nothing more than assuring yourself that the bottom's time is free during the period of intended play. “We've talked,” you might say, “and I have planned a weekend I know I'm going to enjoy. Are you ready to give me that?”

Does music really have a place in the playroom? And, if so, should the beat or music style influence the rhythms and changes in the play?

I find that music can be very valuable in the playroom, and I turn the other half of your question on its ear by choosing the music on the basis of the rhythm and changes I plan for the scene to have. Then, as the minutes of the scene pass, I may be reminded of my plan when I hear the music, but I will not be dragged along in directions that are not comfortable and appropriate on the basis of the play in progress. If necessary, I will manufacture a moment at which to change the music rather than let it change the scene.

Another value music has in the playroom is the masking of the dungeon noises. Depending on the type of music, its level, and the position of the speakers, prerecorded sounds can either reduce the likelihood of others hearing the scene, or be used to muffle the sounds even for the players.

It is also true that some people prefer to play without music. There is, in certain types of scenes, a way in which music overly softens the action, giving it an inappropriate sense of being a planned and mutual activity when, for example, the intent is at least a feeling of spontaneous and even nonconsensual action.

So there are reasons for playing without music, but it usually seems to be more supportive than destructive in most people's play styles.

Questions From Novices

I enjoy rope bondage from the bottom. Now I'm topping more than being topped, but I'm nervous about ropes and knots. What can I do?

Basically, the answer to any question of proficiency is the same: Practice, practice, practice. Fortunately, ropes and knots are easily practiced without enlisting a willing subject who has to know in advance that you are doubtful about your skills. I am reminded of a Sean Martin cartoon, a Doc and Raider panel (I can never remember which of the characters is Doc and which is Raider!) in which one guy walks in on the other who is stringing ropes all over a chair. The one with the end of the rope in his hand looks up and says something like, "Oh, I'm just practicing on my air slave." It's a good idea, but it is not all you can do.

If you buy rope in coils (not hardware store bulk) from some manufacturers, you get a little brochure showing the knots that are most reliable when using that rope. These are nicely detailed, fully illustrated instructions *and you can practice with the leaflet open in front of you* so you'll be ready for the "closed book" test of the next rope bondage scene.

You can also get books about knot tying, some of them excellent. I have even seen a few videos on the subject, but that's really going to extremes.

The truth is that if you can tie your shoes (Okay, boots don't often need tying, but you know . . .), you already know the overhand knot (the base of the shoe tie) and the bow (which is not very useful in bondage, but not entirely useless either). Two overhand knots tied one on top of the other, with the over-and-under pattern reversed in the second one, equals one square knot. Learn that, and you have enough knots to do just about anything. You can reduce the demands on your creativity by learning just one more knot, the traveling hitch (and its obvious variations).

Oh, and then, practice, practice, practice.

Why do some big floggers hurt more or less than some very small ones, even when the same Top is swinging them? I often get to choose the whips that will be used on me, and I'm very often surprised by my own choices.

When bottoms say a whip "hurts" more or less, I guess they mean it is more on the sting end of the scale, as opposed to the thud end. Knowing whether to expect sting (a skin-deep *ouch*!) or thud (a deeper-travelling *Mmmm*!) from a given whip is largely a matter of experience, but there are some guidelines that can be put in print.

Generally, the significant factors are the size of the tails, their shape, and their density. Broader whip tails tend toward thud and thinner ones toward sting. Flat tails are more likely than round (like round-braided) tails to be "thuddy," and tails that have sharp edges (often cut-out strips of rubber or vinyl) or ones that are made of squared-off materials will tend to cause sting. Density is harder to grasp without sample blows, I think. But the word is used in reference to whips exactly as it is used in everyday and scientific language. If a thing or material has more weight per identical unit of space consumed, it is more dense. A one-foot cube of ice, for example, is dense by comparison to (just about anything, including) a one-foot cube of dust bunnies. The more dense a material is, the more deeply thudding its action will be. Compressed leather, as in machine belts and old-style military shoe strings, is much more dense than ordinary, non-compressed leather, and you can notice this when you feel the weight of a handful of, say, flogger tails made of the two types of leather. So, the most painful (sting!) whips would be those with narrow tails that are round or squared off, but the sting will be reduced if the material is denser.

Then, of course, there are all kinds of surprises. Lead shot loading skews the equation, as does the tapering of tails (both of which create faster action, requiring less energy output from the Top, and tending to up the sting quotient). Significantly shorter tails require the Top to work in closer, transferring a greater portion of his energy into the end result of the blow, again, boosting the sting level.

And then there are devious Tops, guys who will use a sweet, thudding, belt-tailed flogger while standing one micron within the range required to reach your back. The broad, dense, flat belts are suddenly reduced to thin, slashing, knifelike edges searing and stinging as they skim past your skin.

Sometimes, there's just no winning.

I have trouble figuring out which flogger to use first, next, and so on. I have some idea of how each one feels, but no confidence that I'm doing the right thing in the right order with my whips. Can you give me any guidelines?

I can share with you the way I often, but not always, compose a flogging scene. Beyond that, choosing the next and next flogger is like selecting and using herbs in a stew, it is personal, creating a style and flavor that come from your own style and sensibilities.

I usually prefer to start with a mixture of rubbing and striking, and the longer I intend the scene to be, the more time and care I put into this foundation phase. I rub with my hands, with gloves, rough mitts, massage pads, or just about anything, and strike with my open hands, the sides of my fists, or a very petite leather flogger. Mixing these around on the fly, I am trying to find the bottom's sweet spots and tensions as I go. Some tenseness can be massaged away, some you have to leave.

Next, I move to either a very soft, flat-tailed flogger or a horsehair whip. If I am going to use the horsehair, I use it dry, letting the bottom's sweat (if any) collect in the hair to increase its density and thud-power. I stay at this level with one or both pieces until I begin to see the general reddening of the back, which I have learned to call "leathering up." This *general* reddening takes place when—often quite suddenly—enough of the back has been stimulated that a broad area of it goes into the defensive mode where the body is dealing with mild trauma, sending more blood to the area, causing very slight general puffiness and, in most people, an overall reddening. [Note: All bodies are different, and some never leather up visibly!]

Next, I use whatever other flat floggers I want to handle, arranging them more or less in order of intensity which is a question to be answered only on a bottom-by-bottom basis. Most bottoms, though, consider that sting is more intense than thud, so we go for the thud first, laying a better foundation for the intense stimulation of the stingy whips to be received well.

Finally, I turn to the more intense braided cats and, lastly, to single-tailed whips.

At every stage, there are opportunities to check whether the bottom is prepared for the next step, and these opportunities can be taken without stopping to discuss them. Counted strokes are a fairly verbal way of getting detailed feedback, but a few moderately intense strokes with the next new whip will usually elicit equally detailed, but wordless feedback. If necessary, you can retreat to the previous instrument for a longer preparation with no loss of rhythm or face.

This sequence is not carved in stone, not even in my own playroom. Every scene is different, even with the same bottom. Every bottom is different. Even if you have seen this bottom responding to what you think was the same scene, it was different because it was not now, not at the end of this day, or this week. Be prepared to change directions for maximum effect for yourself and your bottom. And, until you are completely confident about what you are doing, be willing to give the bottom a way of redirecting your course of action—which can be done without giving up your station as the Top or creating any tendency to pushiness in the bottom.

My lover and I are exploring leathersex, and he recently got a string of 2½" diameter rubber balls that he wants to put up my ass. I don't see a big problem getting them in, but am I wrong to worry about getting them out—especially if he tries to pull them out after I come?

Of course you are not *wrong*. We are, after all, talking about your body! On the other hand, if knowing how other people handle this situation might help you relax about your own capacities, here goes. These "string of pearls" toys are actually easier to put in than take out for many people, but this all changes if you play with the ass hole in question a good deal during the scene. The more pleasant play—whether rough or gentle—your butt gets, the more relaxed it gets. In that sense, the removing becomes easier. On the other hand, if just having the balls inside is all the play your hole gets, there is likely to be a measure of resistance when they are coming out. For a lot of people, getting them out after coming could be a real problem in this situation. The answer then is not to have someone else take them out. Instead, you "shit" them out. If it's hard, push in some lube, and it's easier.

These toys are best used, in my view, as active instruments. They're best if they are in and out a lot during a scene; replaced often with fingers, cock, fist, or something else; eased in at first, but eventually slammed in, until the hole can just about grab them, gulp them, and spit them out without much help. Now, that works! And after a scene like that, coming won't make the balls hard to take out.

I like being told/forced to keep a butt plug in, but I get worried, take it out, then lie (or don't) to the Top, and get away with it (or take my punishment). So, how long is it safe to keep a butt plug in? I wouldn't mind stopping the lying.

As far as I am able to discover there is no safety question

involved with keeping a butt plug in, so long as you don't dam up the exit against the will of your intestinal tract. Don't worry. And, if the result is that you get less of the punishment you want, find another way to orchestrate that. Lying to a Top is not a good habit. In fact, lying to anyone you are playing with, Top or bottom, about anything at all, runs at least some slight risk of causing more trouble than you want to deal with. Honesty may *always* be the best policy, I'm not absolutely sure, but honesty between leathersex partners is absolutely, positively, unquestionably the only reasonable policy.

I don't usually have too much trouble getting what I say I want in a scene, but I have no luck at all getting myself to tell Tops what I really want. Maybe my fantasies are kind of extreme, but they could be safe and sexy, if I could get over myself and ask for what I want. Well, there's the problem. The correct answer isn't just DO IT! I'm trying, and I can't. Do you have any ideas?

It is tempting to say, "Do it!" despite your warning that I shouldn't. Nonetheless, yes, I do have some other ideas for you to try. This may be a case for the personal ads. In an ad you can be as specific as you want, as long as you are willing to pay for the word rate. This doesn't get you immediate action, of course, nor does it get you the same Tops you've been playing with before, unless you are very specific *including identifying yourself* in which case you very well could get the same Tops, if what you want is what they want as well.

Alternatively, you might try writing out a fantasy scene that covers all the points you want to discuss, then you could ask one or two Tops you play with (or want!) to critique the scene. You know, "I wrote this up, now I'm not sure it makes sense or even if it's all possible." Or, "I'm thinking of writing a story like this for possible publication, Sir. Would you mind reading it and letting me know how a real Top would feel about this action." Then, support your own statement by offering the scenario for publication. Why not?

It may even be that you would find yourself able to talk to others about the action you want if you were speaking to "them" rather than "him." Just find a time when you could bring up your real wishes to someone else—maybe another bottom—in the presence of one or more of the Tops you want to get the message to. If you don't get a nibble, you may be on the wrong track with these particular guys and on your way back to the personals, computer services, or bulletin boards.

2

POWER PLAYS

Questions about the leathersex headspace can be very important. Here are the attitudes and ideas that make scenes work, the mental tricks and cues that make it possible to get into a scene, and to feel safe as the scene progresses. Here are panic and self-loathing standing against erotic fulfillment, until you understand how to banish them.

I do it all, anything a Top tells me to do, but I live in constant fear of being told to do certain things. I know I'll do them if a guy is hot and has put together a scene that's getting me high. Is this what it means to expand my limits? I feel like I'm on shaky ground here.

Right enough, it sounds like you're on shaky ground here. It may be more important to you than you realize to *not* perform some specific sex acts. At the moment, it sounds like you are thinking that being a completely obedient submissive is more important than your personal sense of what is acceptable erotic action and what is not. Think about that very seriously.

Your aversion to certain acts, like your preference for others, can be pretty deeply rooted in your self. If your list of "don'ts" is violated, it could result in more trouble than you'd guess—problems with self-acceptance and identity just being the obvious ones. On the other hand, it can't hurt to think about the "no-way" side of your sexual menu, and reconsider.

Just about everyone has a sexual repertoire, based on fantasy and experience, which includes both prohibitions and enthusiasms. Such menus often also include a middle column of things we're curious about and probably willing to try. Experience reinforces our pleasures and confirms our enthusiasm for the things in the plus column. The items in the middle column, once tried, migrate to the left (keepers) or to the right (never agains), and probably don't need to be questioned again. But things that have been in the right/minus/never column from the beginning—untried and unwanted—may need re-examination from time to time. It may be worthwhile to ask ourselves "Why not?" and demand an answer.

Most people will reject certain things on the basis of a real or perceived health risk. Bloodsports of all kinds, piercing scenes, piss drinking, scat, and fucking without a condom would likely fall into this category for many people. And yet, as we all know, people do these things. If they really don't interest you, the fact that others do them and you don't is not a problem. If you really want to do one of these things, or anything on your personal list of taboos, or if you want to be ready and able to do them on command, you may want to undertake some research. Find out exactly what the health risks are and what people do to reduce these risks to levels they consider acceptable. Your informed choices determine the levels of precaution and risk you are willing to take, and these choices should be made at your leisure. Not having the information and, therefore, not making the choices can lead to confusion when, someday, Mr. Right-Now says, "Do it!"

If you have carefully considered your options, and made

informed choices you are comfortable with, you'll be able to stand by your decisions even while writhing under the boots of Mr. Right, much less Mr. Right-Now.

Health considerations are not the only factors to be considered. Maybe you feel strongly that you are, at least in your bottom role, the kind of "scum" a "real man" can and should use any way he wants to. If your dick twitches to that beat, you'll probably do just about anything for the right guy under the right conditions—usually meaning with the right level of power exchange in effect. More likely, you feel something like this "use me as you will" attitude, but with limits.

You may be repulsed, for example, by scat not because of health concerns, but because you "are not that kind of person." You may be able to listen to Mr. Right's explanation of why you should be willing to replace his toilet or toilet paper with your mouth. Then you'll still have to redefine yourself (I *am* that kind of person after all.) or redefine scat players (They aren't *that* bad after all.), or else it's just not going to happen for you.

While it may be that such rethinking can be called expanding your limits, it is also true that your limits have value, particularly the ones you have confronted and decided to set consciously. Not every limit needs to be changed.

What to do then if Mr. Right says "do it" about something that's in your "don't do it" column? Say no. Dress your refusal up anyway you like, but don't let the promise of bliss in the scene at hand lure you into acts that violate your *considered* limits. A bottom is, after all, a full-scale human being, required, no less than a Top, to live with his choices and actions day after day and year after year.

I'm black, and perfectly comfortable with my race and appearance. I don't feel inferior in any way to white men, in everyday life. In SM, though, it's all very different. I'm a switch player, but the power game always has to be black slave

of the white Master, even black slave serving the black "slave-captain." To Top, I "rebel" and turn the tables on the Master/Captain. Does this sound like a racist or self-image problem to you? My friends say it is!

Neither I nor your friends can say with any authority what inner stuff is shaping your sexual interests. You know, if anyone does, and no one else is likely to ever know as well as you, why you find the role of black slave satisfying in leathersex scenes.

Chances are that there is no cause for alarm in this, but you might want to check in with a real authority—yourself. How do you feel about sex, race, SM, yourself, and your partner immediately after a heavy scene in which you have played this role? If you are not satisfied by the sex or SM and/or if you find yourself harboring bad feelings about anything connected with the scene, try to understand why. If you find that you consistently develop bad feelings toward your play partner for no obvious reason, that probably needs attention. If looking at the situation attentively doesn't clear up the questions, you may need either a new play style (unlikely) or some counseling (which won't hurt in any case).

If fantasies of racial inequity are going to be played out anywhere, let it be the dungeon rather than the street or the board room. In fact, if we're going to deal with bigotry of any kind, let it be in erotic fantasies. I learned this early on, when I was still wet behind the ears in every way (except possibly the literal sense). Tops at the SM parties that were my earliest organized experience of leathersex often verbally abused bottoms. Somehow they learned very early on that they lost my attention and my service if they attempted to humiliate me, but I learned some important lessons along the way. I discovered that I was able to see through the whole concept of anti-gay slurs—to discover the fragility and the absolute falsity of the bigoted position—by living through the emotions in SM scenes. Strangely, it was the erotic impulse that became my beacon, the lighthouse on the shore of my truth. What was sexual for me during these supposedly humiliating scenes in which I tolerated being called "filthy faggot" and "worthless cocksucker" was the underlying certainty that my faggot-ness and the fact that I was a cocksucker were *good enough* to be of interest to the Top lording it over me. I am sure that many of the same options exist for black people, people of any other races, for handicapped people, for people who risk being considered ugly, fat, or otherwise unattractive, for people who are especially young or old, and for any number of other classes of people susceptible to bigotry or insults.

My advice about your friends is this: Once you are sure that you are not developing or acting from unhealthy emotions or motivations, tell them so. Say something like, "I know my way of playing could look very bad to you, and I sincerely appreciate the way you alerted me to a potential danger. Now, thanks to your concern, I've examined myself and both the motivations and results of my play. I'm okay. I hope you have looked as closely at your own leathersex style and that you're okay too." Getting more bitchy than that will only give them more excuse to disbelieve you.

I'm white and a Top. I like my bottoms, as I usually say, like my coffee, black and hot. Friends vary in their opinions from calling me a racist to saying that I'm an example of warped reverse-racism (which confuses the hell out of me). I say I'm just playing, nothing more. What do you say?

The Q & A above may be pertinent for you.

I like my boys white, small, not too thin, never over-groomed, and not too noticeably muscular. I have been taken to task in recent years for ignoring boys who are tall, thin as female fashion models, groomed like Falcon models, and very muscular, as well as for failing to play with boys who are Black, Latino, or Asian; fat, old, and very young. I don't want to dissect myself to search for explanations, but I only get hot and hard when I get hot and hard.

I can only fuck when I'm hard and I can only enjoy it when I'm hot.

By the way, despite my stated preferences, the truth is that both of my recent slaves were over six feet tall. Under a very thin veneer of body fat, warren had powerful gym-toned muscles, and I had a live-in lover for over a year who was Black, thin, lithe and effeminate. Love is like lightning, it strikes when and where it does.

I enjoy a certain aura of being forced to perform, of being used and abused, as if it were beyond my control. Is there any way to get that kind of scene under the "safe, sane, consensual" credo we're all supposed to have adopted in recent years?

For me, safe-sane-consensual is not a prescription. It is a reflection. We look at the way we play, consider what works and doesn't, examine our longest-range thoughts and feelings, and we conclude that safe-sane-consensual scenes are what works. The combination of acts and attitudes that is best described by that phrase conforms to the requirements of what I call Rule One of leathersex: Conduct yourself in every scene with an eye to the recycling of the bottom. This means that if the bottom is damaged, deranged, or frightened away, you've done something wrong. You've broken Rule One.

Novices, particularly novice Tops, should give safe-sane-consensual a good deal of respect, even testing their scene plans against it in advance. Experienced players dedicated to Rule One manage just as nicely, and probably feel less intellectual pressure and constraint. For me, Rule One predates safe-sane-consensual by many years with the result that I am far more comfortable with it. The effect is much the same; the mental and emotional gymnastics seem much simpler.

Instead of discussing safety, sanity, and consensuality with *your* Tops, ask them how they feel about Rule One. If they are willing to promise you'll survive and heal, that you won't lose your mind, and that they genuinely expect that they and others will be able to play like this with you again (and that you'll want to as well) . . . well, what more can you ask for?

So, either here and now, or at a later date, you should be able to relax and let your Rule-One-respecting Top do his thing without having to get into lengthy and befuddling discussions of what is safe, sane, and consensual.

None of this is meant to undermine or discard the modern credo. The idea is just to ease up on the preamble to negotiation that is sometimes entailed by speaking the three magic words aloud.

One bottom I used to play with on the rare occasions when I needed something really intense first approached me after a class where I had spoken of Rule One. "I'd be able to give myself to you *completely* any day you're feeling strongly about your recycling rule," he said. I answered that I always feel strongly about it, and would be ready to challenge myself on that commitment the following Saturday. "Want to be there?" I asked.

"Yes, sir. Thank you, sir."

We met, I didn't check in for any more detailed consent, and the result was the first of many intense, spectacular scenes, very satisfying to the "don't ask, don't kill" sadist in me.

I enjoy being a dog. Is it okay to eat dog food if that's what my Master-du-jour is serving?

I'm not very comfortable with "is it okay" questions. The tendency there seems to be (at least sometimes) arranging someone else to blame if things go badly. Dog food eating is a pretty easy question, though, and I'll take the blame if you vomit it back up, but you can take any punishment this evokes.

Yes, eat dog food, why not? Of course, dog food is not health food for humans, and it takes little investigation to discover that not all dog foods are created equal. Despite promises about the food making Rover healthier and more energetic, canine cuisine will not lead to maximum vitality for you if it's all you get over an extended time. Even in the world of born-dogs, table scraps are often part of a pooch's diet, and you should be a good, good dog so you'll be rewarded with such treats as well.

I'm not a dietician, but I play one in the dungeon, and—except for dental pain from badly chosen dog biscuits—I have encountered no problems from guys who will eat dog food. Those who refuse are another matter, and a different set of problems.

Cat food is not the same as dog food! In my experience, some cat foods have thin and dangerous bits of bone in them, or they used to. Cats seem not to mind, but humans might be at risk of damaging their mouths, throats, and other parts of the digestive tract by ingesting these bones. A nurse friend of mine (who doesn't play with animal roles or animal foods) says this is not a problem with "modern cat foods." I say, "Blechhh! Who wants to smell, much less eat cat food, anyway?"

There's no accounting for tastes. And, speaking of tastes, my chef (Me!) has received many compliments on this recipe: Take one cup mashed potatoes, hot or cold, but soft; add one cup of a dry dog food that makes its own gravy; moisten with one bladder full of piss; have Fido stir with his tongue and chin; then, punishing Fido for the mess he makes, let him eat.

If you want to know more about being a dog, check out "My Five Years as a Dog" in *Mach* #6 and "After Five Years as a Dog" in *Drummer* #148. The author, Kai, knows the subject intimately, as you'd guess from his article titles.

What do you do if you want to act out a fantasy that would be wrecked and pointless if the other person knew what it was?

Let's assume you're damned sure the other party to this scene is going to be glad when it happens.

Your best chance of success with a surprise scene is always

to have enough knowledge of the other person (and I am assuming he is a bottom, in this case) that you can get away with springing something on him. To bring this off, you may need a lot of information about the guy *in addition to* his leathersex tastes and limits. For a scene involving abduction and incarceration, for instance, you'll need to be sure he doesn't have appointments, dates or deadlines during the period you intend to keep him occupied. For almost any scene you need to have a *certain* knowledge of any medications the person is taking, if only so you don't get in the way of a scheduled dose. And, as a peculiar aside, you should try to be sure if and when your quarry was last treated to a similar surprise, by whom, and under what conditions. (After all, being kidnaped from the same bar twice in a week may be less thrilling for him than you'd think.)

If you're in a live-in relationship with the bottom, or you play with him often enough, you may be able to just say something like, "Don't make any plans for this weekend. From Friday at six until some time Sunday night, you're all mine." The trust and familiarity of the relationship will fill in the gaps, and set the boy's imagination to work. It may be fun to drop some hints about what's coming up. You could even afford to have some of the hints be accurate.

Nothing inspires a more complete, more rapid, or more erotic connection with a bottom than terror (for the right bottom, of course), unless it is the carefully built-up juice of imagination. So, for a scene that he'd wreck by knowing about it in advance, plan carefully, and consider ways to get the juice boiling before the moment of truth.

A suggestion from my personal history. I once wanted to do a heavy interrogation and torture scene with a bottom I lived with, but I knew it would be more intense and successful for him if he didn't know it was me doing the Topping. I arranged for him to go spend a weekend with a friend, one he wanted to play with, so he was revving up for it. Then I told him the arrangements were for the entire weekend, two weeks away. Actually, the visit was set for a month or more in the future, but my friend helped out by picking up my slave on the weekend I had mentioned, tossing him in the trunk of the car, driving around, then delivering him, hooded and bound, back to my house. I had to do some fairly severe rearranging of things in the playroom to keep him from noticing too soon that he was surrounded by familiar furniture and toys, but it worked wonderfully and was well worth the effort.

I'm glad to have a guy work me over any way he wants to—physically. When the insults, put-downs, and power trips start, it all just seems ridiculous to me, and I can't be bothered. Does SM have to include the insulting and degrading verbal stuff?

Verbal abuse is not a necessity. In fact, it is almost absent from my styles of play.

When I was editing *Drummer*, assistant editor Paul Martin and I discussed verbal abuse many times. He craved it, but often felt damaged or threatened by such scenes much later. He felt that the problem was incompetent Tops, or play partners who were, as he put it, "working out their own stuff instead of playing with mine." I disapproved of almost all uses of verbal degradation, seeing in it the seeds or expressions of all kinds of disorders in both the Top and the bottom.

Later (I was still at *Drummer*, but Paul had died) Race Bannon sent in an article called "Humiliation: A (Possibly) Dangerous Game." [*Drummer* #149] I supported Race's point of view in the next issue by publishing my own essay, "Tongue Lashing Can Really Hurt," and the mail flowed freely. Several letters were selected to represent the various points of view of readers, and they were published as columns in issues 153 and 155. I know you're not likely to look up and read all these articles, but you might. The point is that this subject—humiliation/verbal abuse—is a hot one, with powered-up adherents on both sides.

My take on it has changed very little over the three decades that I have been doing leathersex. I don't think verbal abuse can be done with real safety except in very limited and circumscribed ways. However, if you are playing with a Top who must berate, and you want to learn to live with it, it can probably be done. I know people who seem to manage nicely as "worthless, scumbag, faggots" in the playroom, and adoring lovers between scenes. Still, I am not convinced a really clean and potent power exchange, with all its attendant opportunities and strengths, is ever achieved in a verbally abusive scene.

Is there anything wrong with wanting my slave to stay tied up and watch me use another guy? It's hot for me, but he says it's not SM, it's just cruel. He even calls it rape. What do you call it?

It is not my place as an outsider to your Master-slave household to say anything is wrong with what you do, but apparently your slave thinks something is very wrong, and you must consider that it is at least possible that he's right. Otherwise you wouldn't ask.

I should admit right away that I have had my slaves watch while I use other guys, and even had them assist me while I do it. So, I come down on the side of generally finding nothing wrong with the action. Which is not to say there is no adjustment required in your version of the action.

Even a slave in a Mastered household must be getting his needs met, and must not be suffering from assaults he considers unbearable. If his own needs are being met in every other way, you have only the immediate question to deal with—the one you have asked. If, on the other hand, your slave is not being satisfied in other scenes, he may be choosing this one form of your behavior as the "safe" thing to complain about.

All of that is open to your investigation, and I will assume here that the slave is otherwise getting a life of erotic submission that meets his needs. That being the case, you must now negotiate a settlement with your slave on this one question. The other alternatives are a) to stop what you are doing because your slave doesn't like it (unacceptable), or b) to go on doing it at the risk of losing your slave (highly unacceptable).

Once the relationship is in full swing, many Masters find it difficult to negotiate with a slave. You might need to do something symbolic to set the stage for such a conversation, designing the ritual with a reverse mode to mark the end of the free-speech period. For instance, if you have a framed contract, you might move it to the garage while you talk, and end the talk by sending the slave to reinstall (and reinstate) the contract.

Make the appointment for this discussion well in advance so you both have a few days to sort out your thoughts. Shut off all potential sources of interruption, including the speaker on your telephone answering machine. Maintain only as much of the formality of your relationship as the slave is glad to keep. If, for example, he is normally not allowed to use the furniture, you might ask if he wants to sit on a chair during this conversation.

Try to get the slave to explain in detail what he finds intolerable or disturbing. Don't accept, "All of it!" Find out what "it" is. Is it that he expected a monogamous commitment? Is it that he can't handle seeing your eagerness and satisfaction with someone else? Is it that you do sloppy or uncomfortable bondage on him in your rush to get to your guest? Whatever it is, listen. Don't just let him talk, but really listen.

Then, asking if he has said everything he wants you to hear, take a brief break. Come back from the break ready to tell him what you do like about having him watch you use another guy. Be specific. Check that he is listening. And be sure you are not taking this opportunity to argue with his points. You are not rebutting here, but explaining your own point of view.

Next, if the mood is relaxed enough, explore together what each of you need—as opposed to what you want. Very likely you will be hitting on some points of possible compromise by now. If his trouble centers on the seeing, and your pleasure doesn't depend on that as much as on his mere presence, a blindfold could be one way to improve the situation. If he has a problem with the fact that your guest slaves are strangers, maybe a policy of having him meet them in advance will help ease tension. If he is struggling with being left alone for so long and feels he really needs some attention, you should be able to think of something. Perhaps, just ordering your guest slave to lick your owned slave's dick or feet every hour or so would make a world of difference.

If you both listen, if you both only cling to your *needs*, if the two of you value and want to maintain your relationship, there definitely is a way, and you definitely can find it.

Be sure, once you're back on M/s time, to reward your slave for the efforts he makes to clear things up and keep the relationship on track.

I'm sure I'm not alone in my fantasies: Being used as a fuck-hole, urinal, ass-lick, even an ashtray by a lot of men one after another, or even all at once. Does this kind of scene ever really happen? Can the bottom do anything to make it happen?

Such scenes do happen, although they can be hard to arrange, very hard to pull off successfully, and even harder to keep within the bounds of Rule One (that bottoms should always be left recyclable).

With only the slightest twist of fantasy, however, a boy can create such a situation for himself at an SM party or, with slightly more difficulty, at a sex club. To make this work really well, you have to learn to take some erotic satisfaction from exposing your availability, as well as from actually being used. If you are kneeling by the urinals in a sex club (one prepared to permit such activity, of course), you need to see every man who comes in as an acceptable pisser, unquestionably worthy of pissing down your throat. (Gazing at the men no higher than their ankle bones may help with this.) If you're in the right head space, those who do piss in or on you are no more participants in your scene—your existence as a urinal—than those who choose the cold, white porcelain instead of your gaping mouth. You may talk to yourself about your worthiness/unworthiness to take the piss, but you'll get further if you see yourself as no better or worse choice for each man than any other urinal in the room.

If you're nothing special as urinals go, some guys will be able to take a perverse pleasure in pissing away the juice you want right before your very eyes. Join in that thrill with them.

To arrange a more controlled and different experience for yourself, have a party. Orchestrating the guest list would be hard for most people, but it may be a worthwhile effort. Particularly so since, once you've done the first party of this sort, others will be easier to arrange. Seeing that people at your party recognize you as the ass-lick, urinal, ashtray, or whatever may be another problem. Don't be shy about telling people in advance, and confirming the fact with a sign, perhaps one written directly on your naked body.

If you don't know 50 potential players, start with six. If you don't know six, enlist a friend to help. You might be able to invite three Tops and have another bottom invite three. Voila, a party of eight. This could be especially effective if you and your co-conspirator know different people (giving each of you a few anonymous donors) and if you are friendly enough not to compete for the attention of the Tops.

Alternatively, you could talk to one Top about bringing around several friends. Offer them whatever enticements you are comfortable with. Dinner might do, drinks would be easy, and money may not be entirely out of the question, although it probably brings your intentions in conflict with the law.

I know it seems impossible before you actually start working on it, but it can be done. What is called for here is balls! If you know what you want, sometimes you have to be willing to put your neck on the line to get it.

In Oxnard (Southern California) in the 1960s, there was a guy who was a living ashtray. Cigarettes were crushed out on his body and cigar ashes were broken off into his mouth. There weren't a lot of leathermen or admitted fetishists around, but through sheer determination and courage, he made himself a fixture at many gay parties and cocktail gatherings. There were only two or three houses where the guys I knew in the area got together, and each soon had a table (provided by the human ashtray) on which he would lie still and be an ashtray through every party. Sometimes his hosts decorated him with body paint or flowers. Sometimes they made him wear a g-string or jock strap. But, once his routine was established, no one failed to invite him.

You can get what you want, and you should. Maybe, after a taste or two, you will find you don't want it any more, but you don't know until you try.

I am not humiliated when a Top wants me to lick his boots, kiss his ass, drink his piss, or wear boy toy clothes. Should I pretend it's all humiliating or admit that I'm proud to be able to get a man's serious attention?

I always prefer admitting over pretending, and I hope you do too. Sounds like you could play it either way, though, and that means you can do what always works best in such situations: You can follow the lead of the Top. He may be less accommodating about how the game is played, perhaps even getting a good deal of satisfaction from your apparent sense of humiliation. This, I think, is pretty safe, especially if the humiliation remains nonverbal.

My own preference for behaving honestly in scenes, with no pretending, unless both parties are in on a fantasy, also urges me to prefer straight responses from my bottoms. If I wanted to humiliate a bottom, but my actions only pleased him, I'd move on to more extreme acts, searching for the buttons I wanted to push.

If that prospect is more exciting than frightening, you might want to withhold the pretending with your Top, too. Maybe he'll speed ahead in search of your humiliation buttons, giving you a scene you will find both more intense and more interesting.

I don't know how to feel any more. I think I should be repelled by my own fantasies. Nothing is sexier to me than the image of myself groveling at the feet of an SS officer, begging for mercy, promising to do anything, to allow him to do anything. I know this fantasy is politically incorrect, meaning hard to act on, in any case. Do you personally also think that it is sick, meaning I should seek treatment?

Fortunately, you asked for my personal opinion. That I can gladly give you. I have opinions about everything, and I never leave home without them, but my opinion of this subject is far from universally popular.

Politics have no place in the playroom *except in cases like this* where they increase the erotic heat or up the leathersex ante. If the image of the SS officer gets you hard and gives you access to pleasurable submission, I say go for it.

The only time I would guess there might be something amiss about pursuing a politically unpopular erotic fantasy would be when the people involved were dragging elements of their fantasy roles into their everyday lives. The dungeon SS officer must not expect heel-clicking service at Macy's. That way lies certain madness. But if he can get trembling, kowtowing, groveling service from you in private, why shouldn't he? And why shouldn't you get what gets you off?

Of course, in two short paragraphs I have placed my neck in a noose that many leather community leaders will now want to tighten. I don't mind that. I'll survive. I mention it only as a warning that you might want to be careful with whom you discuss this fantasy. Or, maybe you'd just as soon not pussyfoot around the issue either.

Understand that for most people doing this kind of scene is not a political statement at all. It is a sort of worship scene, but unlike body worship scenes, it doesn't depend on the perfection of the actual person above you, only the perfection of the fantasy (which might depend on a good deal of clothing and props). A scene involving an SS officer Top, a plantation slave owner, an executioner, a cruel animal trainer, or any other wildly unpopular character from the real world doesn't glorify the actual figure from history or current reality. It just makes use of the power imagery symbolized by that person, and power is the very stuff of erotic sophistication.

Sometimes in the middle of a good, hot scene, I panic. Suddenly, I just feel scared out of all proportion to what is happening, and I have to get out right away. I told a friend, and he said he doesn't panic like me, but sometimes he just suddenly feels like the ropes and paddles and "yessir, thank you, sir" is just silly. Are these symptoms of the same problem? What's the solution for both (or each) of us?

I can see the possibility that your reactions and those of your friend might come from any number of sources, but the fact that you present the two scenarios together encourages me to see them as two *opposite* effects of one very correctable problem.

It appears to me that you are both playing with Tops whose scene speed is out of sync with your own. I am drawing directly on my own early experience with leathersex if I tell you that relative novice bottoms can easily experience the irrational panic you describe, and experienced bottoms playing with less experienced Tops are most easily susceptible to your friend's comic-insight problem.

In effect, if a Top is moving too fast for the bottom, increasing the level of sensation too rapidly, or moving from familiar to increasingly unfamiliar forms of stimulation too quickly, the bottom can panic even while being completely clear that the Top is trustworthy and that no real danger exists. The other side of the coin is that a Top who gives the bottom exceptionally long periods between stimulations, or who does not increase the level of stimulation or type of play at a reasonable rate of speed risks having the bottom fall out of the scene the other way, finding the whole procedure silly because it isn't threatening enough or engaging enough.

You may be able to achieve all the "correcting" that is required by telling the Top what is happening, and suggesting the possible truth of what I have just mentioned. Maybe the Tops involved are reading you and your friend to judge how fast they ought to be working, and you're giving mixed or inappropriate signals. It may be that you and your friend should try trading Tops, although that may be very hard for bottoms to arrange. In any case, supposing that I've read the problem correctly, the solutions are not so hard to effect.

When I get into a scene with a stranger or get into one involving activities with which I have no experience, my limits shrink to nearly nothing. Panic is always one breath away. Any suggestions?

My suggestion is that you are responding reasonably, and you should be glad your good sense remains intact during such scenes. Time and experience will change the level of your limits, including the limits connected with new play partners and new activities. Also, you can work harder at settling into the trust you feel which makes the scene possible to begin with. Meantime, being one breath away from panic is enjoyable, too, or don't you think so?

3

THE SEX IN LEATHERSEX

If you're wondering where, when, and how the sex comes into leathersex, you're not alone. Questions on this subject come up pretty frequently, and they can be very important. If the Top and bottom have different ideas about how the sex fits in the scene, their ideas may collide and ruin both the sex and the leather dynamic.

Shouldn't a Top let/make a bottom come just to keep the sex in leathersex?

I don't think so, but you do. Our difference on the subject doesn't matter at all, but if the same difference comes up between you and your play partner(s), that does matter. Sex is one of the things that often needs to be negotiated in leathersex.

Since I know you switch, your question suggests to me that you think you *have to* get bottoms to come when you Top, and that not every Top you play with lets you come. Understand that some serious players—Tops and bottoms—feel they need an orgasm in every scene for some reason. Being permitted (or forced) to come introduces a traditional element of lovemaking, it "spends" the built-up erotic energy, or maybe it's just one more welcome flavor in the sensual smorgasbord. Other players feel that an orgasm gets in the way of what they consider the higher pleasure of the SM play, or they see an orgasm as a too-abrupt stop in their leathersex enjoyment. And, obviously, given a dozen people to question, you could add at least another half dozen lines of reasoning.

There just isn't a should/shouldn't issue here. Instead, there's an opportunity to insert a special pleasure or avoid an unpleasant "bump" in a scene, with no more difficult preparation than a few well-chosen words exchanged in advance.

Leather and sex aren't always related very closely for me. I mean, a good scene can leave me ready for an orgasm, but sometimes I can't come or even get hard after a scene, even one that had no sex in it. Do I have a problem here? If I just say no to sex, will a good Top think I'm a bad bottom? And a related question from another leatherman: **I really get into being flogged and beaten, and I like to be subjected to friction torture and all kinds of pain, but none of it is sexual to me. This is sometimes a disappointment to Tops, or even turns them off. What can I do? Should I try to fake a sexual turn-on?**

The best Tops and bottoms are the ones who learn to communicate freely (getting around any constraints imposed by their roles) and honestly (putting problems, limits, expectations, and potential surprises on the line). Bad bottoms *and Tops* are the ones who fail to learn these skills, and the technical skills that support leathersex activity.

The situation of the first questioner is not the least bit unusual. A lot of leathermen don't mix sex and SM. For a lot of people, the pattern is play till you fall over on the bed and go to sleep, then take a shot at getting sexual before breakfast. Another common approach is for two guys who do SM often with each other to go to others for their genital/orgasmic sex. If you run into a Top who pushes you to have sex when you don't want to, say no. If he can't handle that, you have to wonder what else he'd have trouble handling, don't you?

As for the second question, if it hasn't already been adequately answered, here it is: Faking anything is more trouble than it's worth. Faking most things in leathersex can lead to unsafe situations. Fake nothing. Besides, faking a hard-on is . . . well, not all that easy.

I come too fast, and that's the whole problem. As soon as I know a man is going to take charge, I get excited. At the first move where he actually does anything, I come. Is there a secret I'm missing?

If there's a secret here at all, it's time to share it as widely as possible. When I was young and more excitable (less jaded?), I had a similar problem. I'd sometimes come at the peak of the scene, especially if I were being flogged. This made it hard for me to stay with the action to its otherwise natural conclusion. At times, I was left just struggling to tolerate the decreasing stimulation—which was pretty raw pain at that point—as the flogging worked down from peak to finish. This usually ruined the scene for me, and often damaged it for my much-appreciated Tops as well.

One night, the Top had moved around in front of me, pushed my head back, and started flogging my chest. I came. In no time, I was writhing in discomfort. The Top stopped and put on a bit of an "angry show." Then he ordered the Dungeon Master's slave to get me down, wash me, and bring me to him. I was frankly very frightened. The fear was mostly connected to nothing specific. It was just the law of the parties that all bottoms did everything they were called on to do *to please the Tops*. Before I was delivered to the Top, my fear had fixed on something real: Maybe the worst possible punishment would be invoked. Maybe I'd be told I was no longer welcome at these parties.

Kneeling in front of the Top a few minutes later, all I could do was listen. "This has happened before, hasn't it, boy? No, you don't have to answer, I know it has. If it happens again, I won't. . . ." He broke off, allowing me to imagine what he would not do. Mostly, I thought he might have said, "I won't *just* talk to you." He continued, "Do you know how to prevent this, boy?" I shook my head slowly, now very afraid of breaking the rule against bottoms speaking aloud. "It's easy. Come before you come here." He chuckled a bit, probably responding to the sound of himself saying "come before you come." I thought it was funny too, but I felt no urge to laugh. Then, in a brighter voice, he continued. "My god," he said, "you've been following the rule of no orgasms for 24 hours before the parties, haven't you? Well, don't. The rule's meant to help, not to make a mess of things. If you want to stop squirting on the floor—*and on me* as you did just now—you're going to have to get a good squirt just before you leave home to come here. Can you do that, fella?" I nodded, and he brushed past me to go back into the playrooms.

Problem solved. Permanently.

My most recent slave had a slightly different but closely related problem. Warren would come by the time I got my fist inside him, every time. We got in the habit of playing, even slipping my fist in, until he came. Then we'd shift gears and keep playing, also keeping the play as sexual as we could. Soon he'd start pushing my hand toward his butt, and I'd know we could settle in for an hour or so of happy fisting. If we got the sexual heat high enough in this process, it was even possible for him to come again while my fist was in without having to end the scene.

I don't know any other completely safe way to suppress orgasms than to have had one or more of them very recently. I know some people overdrink, excusing themselves by saying it delays their orgasms. This is not okay for any number of reasons, including the fact that it also suppresses judgment and many kinds of sensual response. Others try to work around their orgasms by trying to negotiate a major decrease in the leathersex action to be initiated when they come, but this puts quite a burden on the other partner. No, coming once is the best way to get *some* control of the timing of the next orgasm.

I want sex at the height of the scene, but most Tops relegate it to the straight time afterwards. How can I work this out?

As I said above, sex is one of the things that needs to be negotiated in leathersex. That is my primary answer.

I'll add two other remarks: First, you say *most* Tops. So, be satisfied with the rest of them if this is a very important issue for you. Second, it is my opinion that physical stamina, control of attention, and access to ecstasy are reduced by orgasm, meaning that deferring sex at least until the later stages of the scene increases the chance of a great SM experience.

For me, it seems there's more love in heavy scenes than in sex. Don't you think that's true?

Love is the yearning of one person for another which inspires each to want nothing more than that the other should be well and happy and growing. Is there more of this in an SM scene than in sex? I think SM provides more opportunity for love to be expressed in *unequivocal* ways we can measure by looking on. But, no. Love is love, and it is no more the province of heavy players than of vanilla lovers. I'd enjoy saying love is more intense among heavy players. I could logically defend that proposition (and probably convince most players), but I'd be lying.

What do you do when a Top wants less sex and playtime than his live-in lover bottom?

I suspect there are few problems more often to blame for the destruction of relationships than mismatched libidos.

My advice is always the same when I see this problem in my own life or anyone's. Don't lose a loving relationship over a sexual difference. In old-style leathersex couples, it was widely accepted that the Top would retain his sexual liberty, playing with and having sex with anyone he wanted at any time. The bottom/slave was expected to play with and have sex with no one except his Master/Top (and, of course, anyone at all that his Top told him to have sex with at any time). This widely accepted ideal rarely works *raw*. But many couples have been able to cook up variations of the ideal which, while doing nothing to diminish the sexual dynamic of the original, work out better over the long haul. The same creative efforts at accommodation can work well for any couple, so long as jealousy is not a problem.

Assuming that a Top who has a more active libido will find a way to work out a solution with his bottom, relying on the traditions of Top-bottom power trade-offs as much as necessary, let's look at the other side of the equation. Of course, what works one direction will usually have a variant that works the other direction between the same two men, even if it requires a different vocabulary to avoid stepping on the toes of sensitive egos.

If the bottom's juices are flowing faster, the possible solutions are nearly endless, and they're all easy (egos and jealousy notwithstanding). Probably the pattern most often tried is one that permits the bottom complete sexual liberty under specific conditions. It may be only when the Top is out of town, which will work if the Top is away often enough. Or, it could be anytime, with notice, and with certain restrictions. The restrictions might include only vanilla sex, only with men known to the Top, only when the Top is home as a back-up rescuer, only at home or never at home, etc.

The trouble with this kind of pattern is that there are often disagreements about the cruising efforts and friendly encounters required of a bottom in order to have someone to notify the Top about and make a date with.

Another entire category of solutions involves the Top making all the arrangements. This relieves a lot of the Top's possible discomfort with a bottom trying to meet and make dates with other men, but it may not work for every bottom. If the Top makes the arrangements, it may involve inviting partners over and leaving the bottom with them, or the Top might stay around and either join in or watch. In traditional leather relationships, the Top might loan out the bottom, or sell his services for some favor from another Top. If the bottom wants the sex per se, and is able to get into the headspace that either enjoys or tolerates the idea of having no choice of partners, this kind of solution can be quite effective. At any rate, it relieves the Top's most obvious worries, while providing sexual outlets for the bottom.

A third whole range of options is based on the couple having scenes in which the bottom gets the sexual release he craves, without demanding that the Top participate erotically. This could mean that the Top orchestrates orgasms for the bottom in scenes that are not so sexual for himself. It could take the form of the bottom being ordered to jerk off at a particular time and place daily (or as often as necessary) whether the Top is around to watch or not. And, more playfully, it could entail the bottom putting on solo, duo, or group sex shows for the amusement of the Top.

For the most liberated couples, secure in their relationship and eager to maintain it without demanding sexual exclusivity or any semblance of it, a completely open relationship is possible. Do whom you want when you want with no other limitations than these . . . whatever they may be, but always including that the bottom continues to be sexual with the Top as often as the Top wants it. A less extreme variation on this worked very well for me and warren for just over a year: He had monthly "Liberty Weekends." During these pre-planned weekends, he could go out as much as he wanted, have whatever play experiences and sex he wanted, and even stay out all night if he chose to. The only restrictions were: first, his liberty should not inconvenience me, which was no limitation at all on him since he sincerely wanted to serve me; and second, he would not go to the homes of men I did not know. This was also a fairly slight restriction. Every time he met someone, he told them he was my slave, that he had my permission to be out, and he needed to know whether the person he was talking to knew me. In the whole year, he only came across one man he wanted who didn't know me well enough to satisfy the conditions of the rule, so they went to a sex club together rather than the man's home. Actually, in the whole year, warren chose to go out on only about six or eight weekends, and did more dancing than fucking on those weekends, but he felt good about it, and was satisfied.

If a couple can't agree on any of these solutions, it may be that they don't really want a solution. Maybe what they are looking for is an excuse to let go of each other. But, if these solutions are not answers, and both parties really want to try to save the relationship, there is yet another approach.

Most men have variable sexual needs. This month or this year, they need sex every day; another time, they're happy with a weekly frequency. This is usually uncontrolled, but it is by no means beyond the possibility of control. The partner currently experiencing the lower frequency need can be encouraged to move closer to the performance level of the more libidinous partner in any number of ways. In fact, many of the solutions mentioned above can have this effect, but it can also be pursued more directly. Two guys watching videos together is the common image of a couple trying to get one or both bodies into a more sensual mood, and it might work, but it seems a fairly lame attempt. After all, a guy who isn't already feeling pretty sexually motivated is likely to see nothing but the ridiculous in a porn tape.

Having the bottom stay naked all the time can inspire lacking urges in a Top. Or, if nudity is the usual at-home uniform, the bottom may add ball weights, tit clamps, or other items of sexual body decor—perhaps only with the Top's permission—to achieve the desired result. Having lengthy periods in which the bottom uses his higher sexual energy to keep himself hard while doing his chores can be a powerful aphrodisiac for a Top, with all kinds of gross and subtle interpretations depending on the dynamic of the relationship. Along these lines, any couple could come up with a few recommendations for themselves that would be better than anything I could suggest.

Then there is the simplest and best solution. Sometimes, once two people know they are having a problem because one of them is getting less sexual attention than he needs, the other finds that—although it is not so important to him—he is able to generate enough interest and activity to turn the tide. At the same time, seeing his partner's efforts, the more highly sexed partner may discover that he can, after all, be satisfied with some degree less sex than he thought necessary. Sometimes, two people turning their attention on a question is all it takes to answer it.

Is it true that I can get drunk and even have a hangover from letting someone give me a wine or beer enema?

I'm sure it's true that you can get drunk and have a hangover from an alcoholic enema. If you couldn't get the buzz, no one would waste even cheap wine on your ass.

A doctor friend tells me that if you want to get drunk and have an enema, you should drink heavily and have a slightly saline water enema. He refuses to explain, but urges me to believe that alcohol enemas are inherently unsafe. My guess: It would be easy to achieve a shockingly and dangerously high level of blood alcohol by way of the digestive membranes in the intestines before the usual fail-safes (passing out or getting sick) could kick in to protect you. My advice: Take the doctor's advice.

I really can't cope with SM—verbal, painful, or Dom/sub—unless my mouth or ass is engaged with HIS cock at the time. But that's not the way Tops operate, necessarily. How do I let guys know what I need without having them label me pushy, or just wander away shaking their heads?

The way to let men know anything is simple: Tell them. One good thing about playing with a number of different guys is that you get a number of different scenes. If I were the Top you told your story to, about 70 percent of the time I'd say, "Fine, message received. Let's go, boy?" The rest of the time, I'd be glad to hear what you had to say so we could both avoid a mismatch.

A pushy bottom is one who insists on getting his way during a scene. What you express as your needs in advance determines with whom you will be playing. If you're polite about what you say up front, it will not define you as pushy.

I admit that I am not the most experienced or oldest leather-man you'll ever meet, but I'm not all that wet behind the ears either. And still I can't figure out the attitudes toward sex I see at bike runs and even SM runs. It seems that the men on bike runs are embarrassed only a little about having sex, but they are appalled if anyone does SM that they naturally know about by the close proximity forced on everyone in the run site. And the men at SM runs seem to generally think that sex-sex where anyone gets a hard cock and does something about it is wrong, just wrong. What is going on here, and am I just misreading what I've seen on the six or seven runs I've attended?

Actually, what you've noticed at SM runs is only a remnant of a much more powerful anti-sexual attitude that held sway throughout the leather world in past decades. And, at a slightly different angle, the same could be said of your bike run observations. Similar effects, but they're historically different.

Briefly, the history of gay male SM extends back to a time— around the middle or late 1950s, later in some places— when many scenes took place between partners who very definitely did not make any overt agreement about consensuality. That would have soured the scene. Instead, what we now think of as SM scenes took place in these circles between a Top, called "a man," and a bottom, called or loudly suspected of being "a queer." The bottom/queer exposed himself to the risk of being beaten and abused by real men/Tops just by going to the bars, docks, and warehouse districts where they were found. Early gay guides labeled these places AYOR, meaning At Your Own Risk, but put the lie to the charade by listing the places at all. Over time, the men began hauling the queers together for parties where less ego-defensive drama was required to arrive at the satisfying effect both wanted. Social evolution has produced many offspring of these early habits— including the modern SM run—and most of them bear some historic apron-strings.

The SM run, epitomized by Chicago Hellfire Club's annual Inferno, shares this history by having been founded by people who either share the history themselves or have inherited elements of it. Sex, particularly sex expressing any sense of intimacy, flies in the face of the underlying history of nonconsensual action. In the 1990s, there may be few people who feel any need to perpetuate the appearance of nonconsensuality to keep their leathersex hot, but there are some. And, if there is any place where the oldest ideals will be defended and protected (often even unconsciously), it is in long-established SM runs.

At the two recent Infernos, the only ones I've attended, I have heard a few people expressing perplexity about the fact that there is so little sex. But I have heard others talking, some thrilled and others distressed, to notice that there is more sex being done more publicly and more "lovingly" than in past years. So, it seems that the grandaddy of SM runs is moving your direction, and I know a few others are doing the same.

This means that unless you run into actual rules preventing it or Dungeon Masters who stop it, you should feel fairly comfortable about having sex at SM runs.

Bike runs are another matter. By the time the earliest SM gatherings had split off or grown apart from the even earlier bike runs, the groups that set themselves apart were already self-identified as gay and self-evidently male. Bike runs, on the other hand, have a history of being male, but not with absolute exclusivity, and not particularly gay (or not particularly "out," anyway).

The bike clubs that have survived the decades are largely gay—with some obvious exceptions—but they have not been overwhelmingly organized or attended by SM players. This is where the distinction between the leather/Levi community and the SM/fetish community becomes important. Some of the earliest bike runs were opportunities for military men to retain the sense of fraternity and appreciation of order they had learned in World War II service. They gladly accepted into their post-war circles other men (and rare women) who respected the values they felt they had fought to defend. Sex was often seen as a disturbance in the fraternal "force," but it was tolerated on a "don't ask, don't tell" basis, which reduced the disturbance.

Recently, I've heard that sex is much, much more public at bike runs than it was even five years ago. What's more, I heard that the one big bike run in California, which has been inching toward SM for years, has actually become comfortably tolerant of outdoor flogging and slaves on leashes in just the past couple of years.

Again, things seem to be moving in your direction. One day, we will see a good deal more sexual liberty at both SM and bike runs, but we must not be surprised if one result of this is some other outgrowth of the fraternal picnic concept, one with more subdued sexuality.

Please, understand that I am not 70 years old, just 48. I can only tell you what I have *heard* about the founding and formative years of the bike and SM runs. On the other hand, when I started going to SM parties in 1964, the Tops were all older men who had a lot to say about these things from their personal experience. They weren't all that talkative to me, a bottom at the time, but some of us remained friends for years, and talked a lot about what was happening around us, and what had happened earlier.

4

ACHING TO PLEASE

Pain scenes are central to the leathersex experience of many gay male players. Not surprisingly a lot of questions are posed about pain itself, handling pain, and the psychological and emotional surroundings in which pain is experienced. What is surprising is the way an understanding of pain can lead to a broader understanding of SM and erotic relationships.

Is there any physical or psychological technique you know for getting past the early stages of a scene where everything is nothing but pain?

Learning to process pain is among the basic skills of the leathersex bottom, and it sounds like you have such a technique in your repertoire. Maybe your personal technique doesn't work so well in the early stages of the scene, or you're playing with Tops who move too fast in the beginning. Either way, I suggest that you don't need to change either the way you work or the Tops you play with. If you're playing with experienced and competent Tops, they may be using this early part of the scene, and knowingly causing you these sensations of "nothing but pain" in the process. Below, I can suggest ways for you to use this period effectively as well, but first I'll explain the way a Top might use it.

As a Top, I sometimes push a spanking or caning or flogging a bit fast in the beginning, usually in spikes of intensity which are very brief, returning quickly to a lower level which I know is tolerable or comfortable before spiking again. In the process, I learn a lot about how a bottom is going to react to the stimulation to come. I also try to become familiar with the difference between his involuntary responses and the conscious and unconscious reactions he seems to be setting up for me to see. This testing period answers a lot of questions for me: Am I playing with a pain-slut who is going to be turned on by the stimulation itself? Is the bottom's assessment of his skill level, as described over time or in the negotiating of the scene, realistic or fantastic? Does the bottom need to be guided into a pain processing method which will give me enough time and psychological space to do a scene we will both be glad to have experienced?

The Top may also be attempting to elicit reactions, and to discover whether you will make adjustments, with the idea of recording (for his nearly instinctive use later) your language of reaction, and your understanding of his responses to it.

From your position in the scene, you could very well be making a corresponding use of the first minutes of pain. You can learn a lot about how the Top plays. In fact, a well-experienced Top will more or less intentionally give you a clear picture of what to expect. You can gather some information about how he will respond to your reactions, and perhaps adjust your reactions to an appropriate "volume" for the upcoming scene.

In general, I'd say that the best thing to do about the relatively unpleasant pain at the beginning of a scene (which is sometimes repeated when the action changes levels or directions) is to learn from it. Your appreciation of the scenes that follow will be greater, and your skill in managing the stimulation will probably grow by leaps and bounds. And that, just in the normal course of things, will decrease your actual discomfort with that early pain while *not* decreasing your capacity to use the raw experience to learn about the Top and the scene that is unfolding.

Am I the only bottom in the world who can only be hit, hurt, or tortured by a man I truly and deeply love?

No, you are not the only one, but I wonder if you are letting this become more of a limit than it needs to be. What's more, I feel it is important for you to understand that not everyone shares your need in this area, and that there is no particular value judgement implied by that. Pain pigs who care very little which competent Top is providing the pain are not lesser creatures than bottoms who have to feel "true and deep" love in order to get into the action. There are different ways of getting what we want, different ways of being who we are, and different ways of establishing an essential element of the power exchange.

An emotional channel must be open between any two players who intend for the scene to feel good, become intense, or get them high. But that channel doesn't have to be the sort of love you are describing. It can even be fairly remote. For example, the need for an emotional link between the players might be satisfied by one or both of them having a passionately pursued fetish and the other sharing or just being fascinated (in a nonjudgmental way) by that passion.

My own sense of things, developed inevitably from my own experience of leathersex, is somewhat different from yours. As a bottom, I felt no need to love the Tops who worked on me. I had to trust them, respect them, and to be unwaveringly willing to have them do what they were proposing. Given the foundation of trust, I was prepared to accept the scene, pain and all. Given the overlay of respect, I was able to submit to the man and the power exchange. And given a solid willingness to go as far as he was willing to take me, I made my emotional connection to the Top through gratitude. All of this was trained into me, I suppose, without my even noticing, and it all worked wonderfully for the types of scenes and attitudes that made up the social web of leathersex as I first encountered it.

As a Top, I discovered that the formula of trust, respect, and willingness was adequate only for relatively simple scenes. As the intensity of what I was able to deliver grew, I found that I was able to perform at such levels only with boys I loved. For me, loving someone means wanting the best for him even if there might be some sacrifice of what I want involved in achieving the perfect experience for the boy at hand. I also discovered, by trial and error only, that I could love guys I barely knew with a surprising depth and passion. I could give them the love I had learned to feel honestly and comfortably without having to promise that I would give it forever. I could, in a sense, love the boy before me unconditionally during a scene (and usually for some time afterwards), and not undermine or cheapen the long term loves of my life.

I had probably never actually understood this before I met Robert Chesley, the playwright famous for stirring up the censors with his *Jerker*. I had noticed a powerful emotional message in his plays before we talked about it. Eventually we discussed it, and he urged me to understand that love could be the connection between two strangers on the street who pass one another without speaking week after week and year after year. He was able to give me an example: A person we both saw frequently on Castro Street had recently died. Neither of us knew him, but the photo of him set up as a memorial in a shop window moved us both to tears. We knew we had come to love him even though we knew next to nothing about him. He was part of the fabric of our lives. Robert cleverly transferred this experience into the sexual arena for me. While I was slow to grasp his message, I have since discovered that most people get it pretty quickly: How much more and more quickly do we love those who are willing to share themselves with us sexually? How much more *in those moments* are they vital to our experience of ourselves? And, perhaps most importantly, how much more do we discover that our intentions are good and even generous toward those who turn to us so intimately? What I learned was not how to love the men I played with, but that I was already falling in love with each boy who knelt before me and that I already considered this a basic necessity for a successful scene of any significant intensity.

Perhaps you have also already learned all of this, and just need to be given the opportunity to recognize and approve it for yourself.

Seems to me all the talk of household items being "pervertible" for SM use is about substitute paddles, and little or nothing more. Got any other ideas?

Ideas? Sure, and memories as well. But first, a warning: I am not there to examine your utensils or supervise your use of them, so I will not be held responsible for your mistakes. Every household item in your house differs somewhat from everything I have, and little differences of design can make a big difference in perverting the item.

Properly cleaned and disinfected, of course, the round handles of ice tea spoons and long, slightly flexible drink stirrers are among my favorite sounds. "Sound" is the correct medical term for a solid (non-tubular) object which, for proper medical reasons, is slid down the male urethra, that is, inside the cock by way of the piss slit. Clothespins and bag-closing clamps come to mind, as well as the padded-jaw clips from skirt hangers. I also remember fondly many scenes in which towels, socks, underwear, and boots have played starring roles when used other than as intended by their manufacturers. Carefully selected rubber bands have been fun too.

Plastic drinking glasses of the relatively squishy kind, fitted with a cord of some sort passing through holes in two sides, can make very interesting gags. Cut a hole in the bottom of the glass before using it, and you have an excellent, washable piss gag.

For abrasion scenes, pervert any of these household items: Fingernail brush, vegetable brush, polishing cloth, emery board, nail file, loofa sponge, pumice stone, sandpaper, and so on. You get the idea.

A phone book, held in both hands, makes an excellent, if noisy, substitute flogger. The dangling handles from Venetian blinds, the plastic sticks you turn to change the light level, are fine canes, but they are likely to break and not be returnable to their usual service. Bed sheets can be used to create immobilizing bondage with very few ropes or very little tape.

Shall I go on?

Use your own native inventiveness to find uses for ice cubes, forks, duct tape, anything small and heavy and hangable, chains, S-hooks, keys, matches, cigars and cigarettes, emergency candles, neckties, belts, luggage, handball balls, rubber hoses, and just about any other household item you can see or think of.

The idea at work here is simple. SM doesn't have to be about leather shop purchases. Starting with your hands, feet, and other body parts, turn your attention to the use of your own clothing and your partners, then let your imagination take you where it will (but with reasonable restraint, of course).

My limits seem to change radically depending mainly on how hot the Top is. I wonder if I'm being overly careful with the less hunky guys, or if I'm letting go too much with the hotter guys. What's it sound like to you?

Sounds like you may have answered your own question, but it also sounds like you may be misinterpreting yourself. It seems perfectly reasonable to me that, to the extent that your SM is sexual, you would be more engaged in the scene and less limited in your action if you are playing with someone who turns you on sexually. Logical, no? The problem, if there is a problem, comes in at the point where you question this fact.

I don't see any need to question it, or to try to change it. There is no particular value in having the same limits with different partners or even with the same partner at various times, so long as you are able to be honest and forthcoming about your sense of your self and your limits every time. If there is a danger here, it could come in two places. First, you might actually be trying too hard to please the guys you see as hotter, and putting yourself at risk by seducing them into going beyond their own limits of skill and experience. And, second, you might be holding back with the less hot men, creating clumsy or dishonest scenes which can become risky.

Without committing yourself to a lifetime of analysis, you can honestly respond to those two possibilities. If you're in the clear on both counts, and you can get guys you consider hot, why shouldn't you? If you're not sure of yourself, work at it. Try admitting to the hottest men that you may be so turned on by them that you might get careless about your limits. The honesty will be read as praise and approval by the Top, which never hurts a scene, especially one with strong erotic elements. On the other hand, it probably would be counterproductive to say to other guys, "I find you rather ugly and unimpressive, so my limits are going to be rather short-fused." No. Instead, you might say, "If I may speak freely, Sir. . . . I'm not sure that I feel up to as intense a scene as we might both like tonight. Can we just play, and see how far we get?" Forewarned, the Top may be inspired to do some powerfully erotic seducing, or he may just accept the limits as he discovers them. In any case, you are covered if you have to stop short of an intensity he may have seen you play at before.

Is the rack just a fantasy translated out of medieval dungeon movies, or can a version of the rack actually be used in SM?

Racks are real. In fact, the most popular dungeon space in San Francisco has a very nice rack. Surprisingly, it gets little use *as a rack*. It is usually used as little more than a bondage frame, holding the bottom in a posture that is helpful for some other form of attention. This does not mean that the players are not engaging whatever fantasies of medieval torture the rack might inspire. My own opinion is that racks are of little use in leathersex *except as sources of fantasy fulfillment*, which can be quite enough for any piece of equipment to do. However, I know guys who have become adept at cinching boys into the rack in such a way that fairly extreme stretching can be done safely, and they find no shortage of players who want to be abused in just this way.

Like most SM equipment, racks require special knowledge and care to be used safely. It is particularly easy to dislocate the joints of the shoulder and ankle on a rack. I have never learned to do the tying in a way that makes me feel safe as a Top when I am stretching a bottom beyond the most rudimentary level. I have, on the other hand, very much enjoyed the level at which I can confidently play with the rack, and I have enjoyed even more the higher level at which I have seen others play. It's just not an important enough or common enough option for me to go the extra steps required to play as intensely with a rack as I do with other toys.

If you are turned on by the rack, you can build your own. In *Inquisition* (the catalog of a 1985, European traveling museum show of torture instruments and art depicting torture; published by Qua d'Arno, Florence), you will find pictures of both the common "table" rack and the, possibly more interesting, ladder rack. If you can't build one yourself from the drawings, you can always use the standard ploy of SM players to get a competent carpenter to make one for you: "It's for a theater project."

I know that single-tailed whips are used on people, but I'm not clear about how. I'm a Top, so I don't want to go under to learn. Is there another way?

It is my view that a Top can learn anything he needs to know *technically* without so much as tasting the same thing from the bottom side of the scene. It is also my opinion that Tops who learn anything without experiencing it from the bottom are very seldom as confident or skilled as those who know from personal experience what sensations they are creating. Clearly, those who have their egos attached to the idea of themselves as Tops will often err on the side of conserving their egos at the expense of their skills. The whole answer, it seems to me, resides in attaching one's pride to the technical and psychosexual skills of leathersex, which would compel (or at least permit) a Top to experience anything in any way which might improve his skills.

My advice, in short, is that single-tailed whips and other forms of play able to inflict damage should be reserved for Tops who have solid experience with them from both sides. As always, I know of exceptions—actually only one in the present case—but I don't approve generally of new exceptions. What's more, the exception I am familiar with is a Top who was already skilled in many forms of pain-giving, who was then trained as a long-whip Top by a bottom who was extremely experienced in that area. These especially mitigating circumstances do not come up all that often, so going under the whip remains an important element of learning to wield the whip. Notice that it is only *one* of the necessary elements. Watching others, being watched by others and listening to their critiques, and collecting the feedback of your practice bottoms are also all important. But the most important element of learning long whips is practice. Practice on pillows, leaves, playing cards, tin cans, feathers, or whatever, until you can hit consistently where you intend to hit no more heavily than you intended to.

The caning of Michael Fay in Singapore in 1994 was quite a source of strange information: a doctor present, someone ready to revive him or deal with shock. What ARE they talking about?

What they are not talking about is leathersex, and that is the important thing to remember. Public caning as a punishment is very specifically not consensual, and it is very definitely not intended to remain within the limits of the person being punished. If Mr. Fay's fate provides a useful source of fantasy, use it as such, but do not imagine that there are leathersex guidelines provided in the television news accounts.

Sometimes the bruises from canings go away pretty fast. Other times they stay a long time. Usually it doesn't matter, but sometimes I need to speed up the process. What can I do?

A friend of mine, Ben, recently told me how he takes control of the bruises by choosing to bathe in hot water (to increase bruising) or cold (to reduce bruising) immediately after a scene. I have no idea how effective Ben's method is, but it pleases him. Of course, his intention is usually to increase and retain bruises, so I doubt that he has tried very hard to reduce or prevent them.

While leathersex players are always my first reference points for information about leathersex, I sometimes refer to outside sources as well. In this case, I looked at *The Doctors Book of Home Remedies*, compiled and published by *Prevention Magazine*, 1990. The advice there is a fire-and-ice treatment like Ben's. The editors, referring to information provided by some pretty high octane doctors, suggest that chilling a potential bruise site with ice helps reduce or prevent bruising. They say you need to start chilling the bruise site right away, and continue for 24 hours, chilling it for 15 minutes at a time, then letting it warm itself up naturally before reapplying the ice. After 24 hours of chilling to constrict the blood vessels and reduce the scope of the bruising, they tell us to switch from ice to heat. The heat, of course, dilates the blood vessels, improving circulation and healing. They also suggest that if it is possible, you can reduce bruising by elevating the bruised area, using gravity to help drain the internally spilled blood from the bruise site.

If you want to reduce your tendency to bruise in a continuous way, the doctors quoted in *Home Remedies* recommend that you take vitamin C. They say you should check with your own doctor before taking major doses of the vitamin, of course, but their suggestion is a usually-safe dosage of 500 milligrams three times a day.

A friend of mine who ought to know adds that bleeding/ bruising is also increased by taking regular aspirin or vitamin E within 24 hours before or 48 hours after the event. So, avoiding aspirin and vitamin E, or choosing to take them, may give you some control of the bruising and marking.

Finally, the *Home Remedies* doctors point out that alcoholics, drug abusers, people taking many kinds of prescription medication, or even aspirin are going to bruise more easily and/or more severely than others. This is based on simple medical facts such as that medications often include desirable anti-clotting or blood thinning effects or side-effects, and blood that flows more readily or more freely means bruises that develop more rapidly and clear up more slowly.

I like cigars and cigarettes—political correctness be damned—and I think a couple of Tops I know would burn me with their "smoking materials" if I asked. Does this have to leave permanent scars? Do the Tops need to know anything special about it to do it safely and "right"?

Tops need to have special information to perform safely and, as you say, "right" in any scene. Also, I believe that bottoms have a responsibility to acquire the same knowledge in order to make informed judgements about Tops, especially judgements that will influence the choice to play or not play with a Top repeatedly.

About the scars: Many bottoms want the scars that come from being burned by cigars and cigarettes, and it is common for Tops to expect that this is the case when a bottom agrees to such a scene. If you do not want the scars, you will have to say so. Given that information, a reasonably competent Top can give you a scary ride on the tip of his coffin nail without leaving permanent marks. You should accept the fact, though, that this is an area where accidents do and will happen. The bottom may move slightly or react a little more slowly than usual and get a little more burn than was intended. A Top may misjudge a reaction or be distracted for a split second with the same result.

Although the risks of real injury in this sort of scene are fairly minor compared to many other ways of producing pain, any scene involving such an obvious risk should be prepared for carefully. This is not the place to undertake the training of Tops for a burn scene, but the training is necessary. Questions you want to have your Top take up with his designated trainer include the following. How long can a hot ash be held against the skin without causing a burn? How close to the skin do we really mean when we say “against the skin”? How is the reaction to a cigar or cigarette end changed by sweat on the skin? How about oils and creams, including lubes? And, how are “natural” tobacco cigars and cigarettes different in the scene from chemically treated ones?

Be an ashtray as much and as often as you enjoy it, but remember to insist that you should be left recyclable at the end of each scene.

I've just discovered that I enjoy being rubbed—hard and long, all over my body—until it hurts. So far, I've only been rubbed with bare hands, but I'm sure there's a lot more possible with this scene. What else do I have to look forward to, and what

words do I use to ask/beg for it?

You have a great deal to look forward to, and you can easily arrange to get more and more of what you want. This kind of action is usually referred to as abrasion, or—rather oddly—as "a sensory/sensation scene." Wander through your own home and give yourself a taste test of potential abrasion toys.

In preparation for this answer, I have just wandered through my own home listing available toys in each room *except my playroom*. Since I like to do abrasion scenes, I have a pretty major collection of toys set aside for these scenes in the playroom. I'll list some of those items a little later, but most of them were found by "perverting" items I picked up elsewhere in my house. I have, of course, also collected a few toys made and sold for abrasion scenes as well.

In the office, I find printer paper, computer disks, and a mailing tube. Sheets of the paper can be crumpled into a ball and used for rubbing, and I could choose to protect the bottom from paper cuts or not, depending how I do the crumpling and holding of the paper ball. The stiff, 3½ inch disks would be excellent scraping toys, and I'm surprised that I have never used them that way before. Suddenly, I'm looking forward to a scheduled weekend next month when a computer-freak bottom will visit. The mailing tube is especially interesting, and not new to me. The end of the tube scrapes interestingly, the sides rub smoothly, and the whole thing is made of cardboard so soft that it will wear down or fold out of the way before it produces any unexpected burns or scratches.

In the bedroom, I find terra cotta coasters molded with a waffle iron-like surface on the top and a rough cork bottom, an old gun (which hasn't had a bullet in it since 1926!) with lots of interesting surfaces and a nice fantasy factor too, and sculptures of water buffaloes made of hardwood, soapstone, and brass. The sculptures provide an amazing array of surfaces, points, edges, and temperatures.

Without carrying this into too much repetitive detail, I notice branches on the ficus in the living room that would be interesting, and I think of rolling up the smallest wool throw rugs and using the thick, rod-shaped roll and the rug's fringe in various ways, and I notice one of my favorite pervertible toys, a newspaper. Several of these items can be used for a certain amount of striking, as well as a good deal of rubbing or abrasion. A few swats on flesh that is being rubbed can accelerate the process, test how the skin is becoming sensitized, and be fun in and of themselves.

In the dining room, I notice a small piece of slate which I have because it preserves the imprint of primordial ferns. Its rough edges and nearly smooth surfaces make it an especially variable toy. My keys are here, and they are old favorites in these games; and there is a small cracker basket on the table. Both the basket and the crackers are inspiring.

The bath is full of toys. A loofa sponge, a fingernail brush, a dry bar of soap, tooth brushes, combs and hairbrushes, a tiny moustache comb (good for getting into otherwise inaccessible private spots), a rough washcloth, and a set of tools made for dental scraping all look worthwhile.

In the playroom, I have several kinds of bumpy-surfaced gloves, ranging from rubber bathing gloves to rubber-studded curry gloves and "vampire gloves" (leather pads and gloves with pin-prick studs) made specifically for this kind of play. There is a collection of brushes, ranging from a soft shaving brush to very stiff brushes made for cleaning vegetables and one made for scrubbing floors.

I could go on and on, but the idea here is for you to get up and take a similar tour of your own home. Then, there remains the question of how you'll get a Top to use your discovered toys on your waiting body. Simple: Ask him to do it! You might need to couch your request in a way that makes sense in the context of your relationship, but you can work that out. Tell him you "noticed" that this brush or that cloth produced an interesting sensation, and you wondered if that might be something he'd like to add to his arsenal. There's no lie involved because you certainly would notice the sensation when you taste-tested it, and you'd certainly not be suggesting the instrument to him if it were not at least interesting.

Few scenes offer as much room for wildly creative imagination as abrasion scenes do. So, get creative and imaginative. Then, once you get the ball rolling, don't be surprised if your Top(s) come up with their own ingenious touches.

I can't seem to get the lights right for flogging. Behind me, they cast confusing shadows; in front of me, they're in my eyes and the bottom's; at the sides, they get in the way of the whips. What do you do?

What I do is not going to be an answer for everyone, but I don't mind at all sharing my solution with you. For the reasons you mention, I found that it was impossible to handle a whip decently with light coming from behind. So, I have my playroom set up so there is no light at all coming from directly behind me. Over my right shoulder, as high as I could put it and as far out to the right as possible, I have installed a high-intensity lamp (the kind meant to be used on a desk). Rather than giving a sharply defined circle of light as it is intended to do at close range, the high-intensity lamp at about 10 feet from the bottom's back gives a clear, clean, and very white light on the back without flooding the room with unwanted general illumination. The rest of the light comes from two sconces which are installed on the walls to the right and left, about 12-15 inches behind the plane of the bottom's body. The sconces are on a dimmer which is near enough to me that I can turn it up and down without interrupting the scene. There are no light sources in front of the bottom, and the sconces—although technically in front of me—are far enough off to the sides that I have no problem with them.

The description above may make my playroom sound much bigger than it is, and encourage you to disregard my plan because you think you cannot duplicate it. Disregarding the part of the room not included in a flogging/whipping scene, the area I am working in is about 100 inches square, or about 8' 4" on each side. This is an acceptable space for most flogging, but a very small area for most single-tailed whips. I get the high-intensity lamp ten feet away from the bottom by having it within an inch or two of the ceiling, in a corner. As I suppose is the case with most people, I'd like to have a larger area and more lighting options, but this has worked nicely for more than four years.

I love to have my back flogged, whipped, paddled, and beaten, but I just feel irritated when a man wants to spank me or whip my ass. Does this make sense at all? Should I be trying to change it?

Ah, there's that word again, "should," and it gives me the usual buzz of discomfort. As a Top who likes to have maximum freedom about where and how I use the bottom's body, I wish every bottom had approximately no opinion to express on the subject. On the other hand, it is your body, and—much as my Top side wishes to deny it—the pleasure is intended to be at least partially yours as well.

My slave, warren, arrived already fond of having his butt severely abused, but he was of the opinion that striking and flogging his back was a discomfort he had to bear to please me and his previous Tops. I accepted the gift of his back eagerly, and he soon learned to like what I did to it so much that he often asked for floggings that he would originally have tried to squirm out of. This only proves that, even if you do not set yourself the task of changing your feelings on the subject (as warren did not), things sometimes change for other reasons.

My previous slave, scott, found that he handled back beatings pretty well, but became too connected to his personal history of unwanted childhood spanking if his butt got hit with anything at all. The result was predictable. There was nothing erotic about spanking or butt flogging for him, and it often left him feeling unfocused anger. This never changed, although we "checked in" from time to time, both of us hoping to discover that our relationship had replaced his memories in this connection.

So, know that you can make changes, but understand that there is no reason to do so unless your current limitations are standing between you and pleasures that you really want to get to. No one likes everything.

I like to drip candle wax on guys, especially on their hard cocks, but they usually can't handle it. I've dripped a bit on my hand, and it's not so bad. I know hot wax is a "standard" scene, so why can't I get away with it?

A Top can generally get away with anything that is within the bottom's known or desired leathersex territory *if he knows how to do it well enough.* I can only guess that you don't hold a candle to your bottoms the way they want it done. It also sounds as if you are failing to check in with the bottoms after the scene goes awry.

Take it as an absolute rule that when you have a scene that doesn't work, you must find out what about it didn't work for your partner. Even if the scene hobbles along to something like a conclusion, if you know it wasn't working as intended, find out what your partner believes is the reason.

What are you likely to discover if you have the balls to ask the bottoms you've tried to wax about their experience? Maybe they'll say you moved too fast for them. I find that hot wax works best as a slow and rhythmic scene with surprise pains and an escalating level of overall sensation. The way to control the level of sensation is obviously to control the quantity of wax being dripped, and even more importantly, the distance from which it drips. The tiny fractions of a second added to a drip's falling time, represented by a few added inches, can make a remarkable difference in what the bottom feels.

Your bottoms might say that you don't seem to know what you're doing, then very possibly be unable to be more specific. If this is the message, I'd guess that you are not being appropriately responsive to the differences in sensitivity of various body areas. On a hard cock you have several areas of extremely different sensitivity, each of which needs to be investigated with expeditionary drips as the scene progresses.

There is, fortunately, an easy way to learn to handle hot wax: Do unto yourself what you hope to be allowed to do unto others. You don't have to put your ego or reputation on the line to wax your own dick. You can do it in the privacy of your own play space. And, I'll bet, you'll figure out pretty quickly exactly what you're doing wrong. Maybe, being a Top, you won't enjoy the experience (there's no reason why you shouldn't!), but you'll discover what feels different from what, what hurts and what is potentially manageable sensation.

Actually, I find myself wondering if you know that there are right and wrong candles to do your dripping with. Just in case, I'll tell you. Do not use beeswax candles, candles with wires in the wicks, or ones that are made with a lot of added chemistry to harden them, prevent them from dripping, help them hold bright colors, or cause them to burn with a brighter or prettier light. Do use paraffin candles. The easy way to distinguish the good candles from the bad is to look for "emergency candles," which are usually just molded paraffin with a string wick. What's more, the right candles are almost always the cheapest ones you can find.

I enjoy electrical play and use a TENS unit, but I'd like to know more than salesmen in stores can tell me about butt plugs, cock rings, and other attachments. Violet ray machines,

too. Where can I get reliable, informed help?

Reliable informed help in any scene is, under perfect conditions, a product of friendship. There was a time when SM players jealously guarded technical information, doling it out to friends as a benefit of increasingly intimate friendship, trading it at times the way kids trade baseball cards, and often withholding information as a way to maintain a position of respect or significance in their circle of acquaintances.

These days, information is shared much more freely. There are books and pamphlets, classes and demonstrations, and sometimes even hands-on instructors available at dungeon parties.

I won't attempt to explain the broad area of electrical play here, but I can suggest that you must have a few friends who have information you could benefit from. How about the people you have already had electrical scenes with? Some of them might also have had scenes with other electricity players, and they will have something to say about how these others played differently than you do.

This is also an area where I know a number of people have used personal ads successfully. A friend in Arkansas wrote that he had no one nearby to teach him about electrical scenes, but he wanted to learn. I couldn't go to Arkansas, and didn't especially want to be the one to teach him, anyway. So, he ran a personal ad in *Drummer* asking experienced players to get in touch with him. His intention was to exchange letters with a number of people, learning what he could from each correspondent. What happened is that he had responses from about six people within an hour's drive of his home, one of whom even had a nicely equipped, all-electric playroom. He kept up his correspondence with others who wrote, but ended up being more the instructor than the student with most of them because he was getting lots of locally-available, hands-on training.

How do you control yourself when a bottom is begging—even in so many words—to be devastated and injured? I like to go as far as I can. I come when a bottom screams for mercy and is really hurting, but there must be some way of stopping the progress without ending the scene. Isn't there? Obviously, I haven't found it.

I am not inclined to think of anyone in the scene as sick or in need of professional help since I believe there are always ways to get what we want *safely*. Nonetheless, I suggest that you think about this question for yourself: Do you need professional, psychological help? If you are unable to answer with a powerfully definite no, then you should at least discuss the question with an SM-friendly therapist of some kind.

Supposing you are not as out of control as your question suggests, and that a little technical advice will fix the situation, read on.

There may be many ways to deal with your problem, but the easiest one technically may be both the most effective and the hardest one for you to accept. So that's the one I'm suggesting. Generally, I have discovered that Tops like yourself will do just about anything to avoid giving the bottom a safeword. Get over it! Give every bottom you play with a safeword, and make yourself believe in it. Meditate on this safeword if you think it will help. Do whatever you have to do to make it important to yourself. After all, without it you will eventually be reducing the number of bottoms willing to play with you to the inevitable zero.

If you can accept the idea of the safeword (and, really, you need it more than most Tops), you might still have trouble with communicating the safeword. You may feel there are implications to that part of the discussion of the scene that undermine or lessen your power or authority. There are bottoms who would agree with you, but playing with these "no limits" bottoms only increases the importance of the safeword. Solve the problem simply: Choose one safeword and use that word in all scenes. If you can't talk about it, have a professional quality sign made and post it at the entrance to your play area. When a bottom arrives for a scene, even if you are dragging him in, you can certainly stay in role and in power while saying something like, "Read that sign there, boy. It's the last you'll hear on the subject, and you better not forget what it says."

What does the sign say? Maybe it says, "I work HARD in this room. If you can't handle it at any point, say so. Say, PARDON ME, SIR! No other complaint will be listened to!" This particular version of the sign presumes a *verbal* safeword. With a little imagination, you can adjust it to something nonverbal. For example: "I work HARD in this room. Before you go in, pick up one of the black balls from the box below. If you need to escape at any point, drop the ball."

In a heavy scene, I almost always start crying. Some Tops are shaken by it, others are not. I don't know how to feel about it. How do you see it?

I like it, and it doesn't sound like you are personally disturbed by it. To me, getting a bottom to cry without having to stop the scene is *sometimes* an achievement.

If you're concerned, or if you have been playing with Tops who give you the impression that they are concerned, just deal with it up front. Before the scene begins, tell your man the truth about your crying, and listen to his reaction.

Maybe you feel that crying is a sign that the scene is going well for you. Maybe you feel that crying indicates that you are connecting well with the Top emotionally. Maybe you feel that you are close to your limits when you cry, and it may mean that you don't want to push on, or *that you definitely do want to work through it.* Tell all, but keep it very brief. One sentence is sure to do the trick.

If the Top is going to be bothered by your crying, ask him for a gag and blindfold so he won't have to be aware of it. Or, if you think you can do anything about it, promise him that you'll *try* not to cry.

I don't see a problem here, but if it seems distressing to you after enough repetition, it may suggest that you are connecting with emotions or memories that you'd be wise to explore. A friend is probably as good as a pro (at least to start with) if you want to talk about what internal stuff the crying is attached to. Be prepared for the possibility that you'll want a trained counselor or therapist if you're coming up against things you want to resolve that way.

Please, do not get the idea that leathersex is the therapy you need. This attitude and all its implications are dangerous. Therapy is therapy, whether it happens between friends or between a person and a hired professional. Leathersex is SM and sexual activity whether it happens between friends or between a person and a hired professional. The potential pros in these two scenarios are trained in different professions!

Once you get past whatever problems you may be having with Tops over your freedom to cry, you may want to think through what the crying means to you. If it is a relief of stress, is that okay with you? If it is just part of the mechanism of your submission, do you mind, or might you want to see if you can find other ways to achieve the same thing? Or is crying truly a cathartic experience for you, something you have every reason to value highly?

Is a bottom supposed to scream and howl when he's tortured? I feel better grinning—or usually not—and bearing it in silence, but this bothers the few Tops I know.

Different people feel very differently about the verbal reactions of bottoms to pain or torture. This, like most elements of a scene, can be negotiated. Unlike most other elements of a scene, this one can be safely ignored between most pairs of players. If you discover that the people you are playing with are misinterpreting or being bothered by the kinds of sounds you make, clear it up by talking about it. Even in the midst of a scene, you can probably say what needs to be said. If not, talk about it later, but keep it simple.

What do I do when I am Topping and I suddenly see that the bottom's limits are more advanced than my own, that he can take more than I can comfortably give?

You still do exactly what you can honestly and confidently do, and nothing more. If the bottom is more experienced, it does not follow that he has lost his capacity to enjoy and appreciate what less advanced players do.

I don't seem to get much out of being tortured or hurt, but I can almost never come without imagining I'm being brutalized and even hurting myself a little. Is there a way to find out what I really want, and to get it, without putting myself too much at risk of either being hurt badly or embarrassing myself and disappointing a Top?

There is always a way to get what you want or need in leathersex, even if what you have to get is a clear idea of whether you really want leathersex at all. You can easily enough arrange to go to an SM play party [This question came from a man in New York City.] or you can go to a leathersex club where you will have to explain your situation carefully to potential Tops willing to listen. Trust me when I tell you that there are players out there who will be sympathetic to your situation, and glad to help you through your explorations. Bottoms who sometimes Top may be better bets than men who identify themselves as exclusive Tops, but you never know.

For guys who share this problem but don't live in a city where there are so many options for finding potentially cooperative partners, it might be possible to draft a friend who is willing to do some experimenting with you even though he may have no special interest in leathersex himself. This can be a little more difficult, and you will not get such a comprehensive answer, but it may be enough.

If you come to the conclusion that your fantasies are enough, accept that. There is no reason to push off into the sea of radical sexuality if fantasies related to it really are satisfying for you. Similarly, there are people who find that their radical sexual needs are best satisfied by solo SM in which they provide the bondage, pain, or whatever for themselves. Both of these options have inherent dangers, but they are obvious enough to be easily avoided by reasonably intelligent fantasy or solo players. In fact, the only concern I have about either group is that they could become so fascinated with their own skills—whether imaginative or active—that they lose touch with others sexually. I would consider this unfortunate. You may not.

5

BONDAGE AND SENSUALITY

Pain scenes make up the famous and feared portions of leathersex, but I suspect that bondage and scenes involving stimulation in the range of the sensuous make up the bulk of leathersex experience for most men. Questions about bondage and sensual scenes tend to be more about tastes and opinions than urgent matters of safety and sanity, but some of the questions below prove that the problems can still be important.

I like getting tied up, but guys tie me up then hang around to spank my butt or something. Don't Tops know that we bottoms want to get tied up really well, then left alone for a few hours?

Take a look at the question below.

I like getting flogged, spanked, clothespinned, and otherwise played with, and bondage is fine with me, as a part of just

about any scene, but I don't have any idea what could be interesting about JUST being tied up. Do you?

Very few things are as difficult as understanding someone else's erotic trip when you don't already share some significant part of it. One thing comes to mind that is harder than this understanding. That would be *doing it*.

To begin with, it is always a mistake to suppose that your own preferences are universally held, even if you know no one who disagrees with you. There may be some few general statements that can be made about gay people, men, women, bottoms, or Tops which would seem almost universally true, but all you have to do to find exceptions is to behave as though there are none.

As to the specific questions here—what's the turn-on in just being tied up? and how can you get a Top to just tie you up and leave you alone?—the answers are really pretty easy to come by.

Some people are turned on by bondage *per se* and others enjoy bondage as part of a scene that is centered on something else. The bondage in both cases has the same erotic wiring: It establishes and confirms submission, it reduces free use of the will, it relieves the person of all concern for bodily movement and the use of the body, and it connects him to the inner pathways which define him as a leathersex player and (at that moment) a bottom. The bondage underscores or even engages the erotic nature and identity of the bottom, and encourages him to focus on his accessibility to forces that are either outside himself or, if inward-sourced, not usually free to act.

Stated in terms like the ones I just used, bondage doesn't sound very sexy, but I could just as well describe the workings of any scene in the same way. Besides, the description of any turn-on stated in terms that reflect the excitement it engenders will zip right past people who don't already *feel* the buzz. But here's a sample, anyway: Bondage works for me when I feel the control I usually have to exert in my life passing to someone else. He, not

I, will be responsible for me and my safety and how my body is used until I am released from the bondage. He must watch and think and know; I am free to be, with no other demands or requirements. Where I go when I am freed in this way is beyond description, but it is a state in which everything that I would usually find troubling is laughable, or forgotten. To be bound is to be free of everything except the single most rewarding thing a man can do, being himself without definitions or boundaries.

There is the high in bondage, and that turn-on—lessened or diverted one way or another—is what makes bondage during other kinds of leathersex valuable to the bottom. (Note: A Top may have specific practical intentions for tying someone up, or he may absorb the dominant's version of the submissive thrill described above. Or, at best, both.)

While I believe I have now answered why anyone would want to be "just" tied up, I am well aware that no answer will cause a person to suddenly desire bondage for bondage's sake. The other question, how to get Tops to leave you alone once they tie you up, is much simpler.

Negotiate what you want. I know, I know . . . this concept of talking about scenes before they take place is disturbing for a lot of people. It seems to dampen the excitement for some folks, but is it really worse to have to mention what you want than to have to live without it? Furthermore, you can sort out potential partners a great deal in advance, to reduce the need for discussion; and you can do the negotiating in advance as well, to greatly reduce the need for discussion immediately before the scene.

In the present case, for instance, you can look for people who are specifically interested in bondage. That might involve watching for light grey hankies hanging out of left rear pockets, cruising the personal ads in a very specific publication like *Bound & Gagged*, searching your personal network of friends by telling everyone you know what you're looking for, and shopping on computer and telephone lines with your preferences always boldly stated. Once you find possible partners this way you have reason to believe that they are interested in bondage, the type of bondage that you want, and that they are in a position to understand (or, at least, to have previously encountered) your hope that you will be left alone once you are tied up. The more up front you have been about this in the cruising and shopping phase, the less refining you will need to do on a more personal level.

Once you reach the one-on-one stage of communicating about the scene, you should be able to say exactly what you're looking for in very few words. Be prepared to accept some tit for tat here. To take an example I am familiar with, I find that it is necessary for me to have played with a person a number of times before I am willing to commit to a lengthy vigil while he stays in bondage and untouched. So, to get a long, bondage-only scene from me, a guy has to see me several times, and accept that I will give him increasing, but not unlimited bondage periods each time we play. Also, while I am willing eventually to do the bondage-only scene, I want some other kind of play in the earlier scenes. The additional play may be slight and simple if the guy really turns me on and I am looking forward to the longer bondage scene myself. Or, I might be moved to give a bottom the bondage scene he wants later if he'll give me his back for a flogging scene (and some bondage) now.

Everything is possible with the right partners, and no matter what you want, someone is out there looking for the complementary role in the same scene.

How long can I stay tied up without being hurt by it in any way? I don't mean that, exactly, but I don't want to be damaged by bondage. Do you understand what I need to know?

You can stay in bondage and completely safe from damage as long as you are completely comfortable *plus about 15 minutes*. That answer is meant to be neither flippant nor mysterious. Some forms of bondage may be completely comfortable for a very long time. I have left guys, properly catheterized and otherwise taken care of, in bondage for more than 24 hours. At other times, using similar bondage methods meant to last for hours, I have had to take guys out of bondage on very short notice after only minutes. Once body parts begin to complain, the bondage must either be removed or adjusted, unless the pain being presented is intended and controlled by the Top in charge of the scene.

Of course, there are some far outside limits that ought to be considered. Keeping a man tethered to a wall by a steel collar and chain can certainly be considered bondage, and it could go on for a very long time. Eventually the body will accommodate the collar by developing callouses to keep it from further damaging the soft tissues or threatening the bone. You have to consider for yourself whether the bruises, torn skin, and perhaps reshaped bone structure that lead through the months to the callouses are damage or just the way the scene progresses.

On a more realistic scale of, say, overnight to through-the-weekend scenes, the types of damage that can result from bondage are generally pretty obvious. Bondage that interferes with circulation, breathing, or elimination of body wastes comes with risks best understood in terms of those effects. Circulation to different body parts may be altered or reduced to varying degrees with quite different results. Brain damage, for instance, can take place very quickly if blood doesn't flow freely into the head, or if breathing is too severely restricted to permit a more or less normal oxygen exchange in the lungs.

As you see, without writing a complete medical text on anatomy, it would be impossible to catalog all the possible risks and how to avoid each in long term bondage. Hence the rule: You may stay tied up as long as you are completely comfortable—free of panic, pain, and physiological pressure—plus about 15 minutes. Then the warning beyond the rule: Some people and some body parts cannot bear the discomfort for the 15 minutes.

Once, a guy had me all wrapped up—the word mummified makes my skin crawl—and he rubbed some kind of grease or lube on my balls. For the next half hour, I was in heaven, dealing with the blazing near-pain from this grease. I know, because I've tried it on myself, that it wasn't oil of cloves. Friends tell me not to even try alcohol. What was it?

It seems most likely that your friendly neighborhood Top greased your balls with any one of several medical gels and creams that are meant to relieve muscle strain and local pain. My favorite is a Bristol-Meyers product that promises to relieve arthritis pain, simple backache, and muscle aches. It works pretty well as intended, but it's dynamite used as you describe. The product is called Mineral Ice. There are others called, generically, chiropractic ices, chiropractic gels, deep-cold salves, and cold-heat creams, but Mineral Ice is available in most pharmacies, and some of the others must be purchased from either health food stores or chiropractors. You needn't be embarrassed when you go to buy any of these products, even if you have to ask for help finding them. People of all ages, genders, and sexualities use the stuff legitimately. And, if you're up to it, play dumb. Ask the pharmacist for help in locating Mineral Ice (even though you may have seen it featured on the shelf), and tell him you wish it lasted longer, or got hotter, or whatever you may wish. His advice may lead you to an even more effective product for your special need.

I didn't mention Ben-Gay or Deep Heet because, even though I know they are used, I don't like them. I have had experiences where the bottom suddenly felt a need to get the stuff off, and the penetrating preparations just don't come off. Besides I (and others, no doubt) dislike the smell of either of these medicines, but don't mind the varying mint or spice scents of the chiropractic products I use.

One last note on this subject: The person who applies these delights should wear disposable gloves. It isn't that the Top can't bear on his hands what he puts on a bottom's balls (but why should he?). It is a matter of being sure the gel isn't accidentally transferred to mouths, eyes, or any other body parts where it is dangerous or unwanted.

I'd heard that heads-down suspension could only be done for a few minutes at a time, but I just had a scene where—at my request—the few minutes got extended to nearly 45 minutes, and I was still fine. Am I all that different? If so, how am I different? If not, am I hurting myself in ways I don't know about?

To a certain extent you are up against the leathersex-instruction version of "do as I say, not as I do." There are any number of scenes for which the commonly taught warnings and limitations are preposterously cautious, to say the least. This situation is unfortunate, but also unlikely to be remedied so long as we live in a society of blame where lawsuits are everyday affairs, with defendants being dragged from the farthest reaches of potential responsibility.

Most of these outrages of reality in the name of safety can easily be overcome by your own experience, and the lie is put to any number of them by simple logic. Nonetheless, every player has to be left to make his own discoveries because of the *aforementioned, hereinafter called sad, litigious social situation.*

Speaking of simple logic, it answers your question directly. If it were generally true for most players that upside down suspension could not be permitted to last for more than a few minutes, then there'd be a lot of damaged yoga fans out there. Sometimes—in the pursuit of improved psychological, spiritual, and physical health—they stand on their heads for much more than "a few" minutes.

The final cure for overcautious safety warnings is for you to set up the most comfortable and safe conditions you can for the kind of scene you want to learn. Then, monitoring those safe conditions carefully, explore what is actually possible and desirable for yourself. Experience is the best teacher, and it makes of you your best advisor.

I like to have ripe pits ready for raunchy licking at night whether I'm stretching my own nose and tongue out for the treat or I find some boy who wants to pit-dive. Do you know any way to have ripe pits at 10:00 PM without turning the stomachs of my 9 to 5 co-workers?

Your personal body chemistry and dietary habits have a lot to do with what will work for you here, but let's take a shot at possible answers, anyway. Besides genes, the factors that determine body odor are diet, perspiration, bacterial growth, and your clothing. It may take a while, and a good deal of experimenting, but by working on each of these factors, I'm sure you can come up with a combination that gets the job done to your satisfaction.

I'll be mixing advice based on personal experience with facts culled from *The Doctors Book of Home Remedies* (by the editors of *Prevention Magazine*). First, let me lay out the assumptions I am working on: a) you are starting from only normal body odor rather than a particularly pesky problem that haunts you all day; b) a solution is worth a certain amount of effort; and, c) you have access to relatively good reports, other than your own, as to what scents are being emitted both at work and in the evening.

Step one: Do not use any deodorants, deodorant soaps, or anti-bacterial soaps or scrubs. All of these, for our purposes, are overkill, meaning they'll kill off the bacteria which help to ripen your pits. In fact, without these helpful bugs a reasonably clean person may find he just doesn't generate any of the nice musk we are looking for.

Step two: Try doing your basic bathing or showering at bedtime rather than in the morning. This, if it is possible, will give your bugs longer to work up their vapors before the next night.

Step three: Keep raw garlic and raw onions to a minimum. The scent they can sometimes give your sweaty areas is not the one we are looking for, and it is thought that they (especially the garlic) kill germs. Besides, strongly flavored foods in general tend to lend their own tones to body odor for hours, throwing the manly musk all out of balance.

Step four: Wear only natural fiber shirts to work. Fabrics that are all-natural, cotton more than most, will absorb the sweat and allow it to evaporate bit by bit all day. Other shirts, which might be more useful for building up a stench on your days off, trap the sweat and encourage the development of the bacteria that like dark wet places. Sounds good, no? But, for the purpose of having odorous pits by 10, without scaring people all day, the cotton will be better. This means both cotton T-shirts and cotton outer shirts.

Step five: If it seems necessary, use a little camouflage for the daytime hours. Hunters use pine tar soap to mask their human scent from the superior noses of deer and the like. So, having bathed last night, get up this morning and wash your chest and shoulders—but not your pits—with pine tar soap. You should give off a pleasant pine forest scent for many hours, and you can use a hot rinse with a wet wash cloth to finish off the trees and let the musk shine through after work.

Step six: Get excited and active after work. Sexual excitement, fear, and strenuous exercise all lead to sweating. With sexual excitement you pitch the pheromones (subtle scents of sexual desire) into the mix. With fear you toss in sharp or bitter overtones which may also be acceptable. On the other hand, it's kind of hard to arrange to get frightened every day after work, and the kind of sexual excitement that will get the juices flowing is not usually a solo game. What's left is strenuous exercise. Walk home, get off the bus two or three stops too soon, and take a jog after you get home. And, to improve the effectiveness of the jog, wear a spandex or latex tank top under a polyester shirt. Now, you can up the ante a few more notches by not laundering your after-work togs too often, and maybe hopping into the jogging outfit at (or near) work so you can get an early start on your bug cultivation.

Final step: Wearing anything but your natural fiber work clothes, chill out for a while after you sweat it up. A little sweat given a nice, long, arms-down ripening phase will get you where you want to be better than gushing wet sweat right up to the moment of truth.

I'm into feet, but not boots. Just about any non-boot footgear can turn me on, some more than others, but boots don't get it. They seem pushy and arrogant compared to Bass Weejuns or wingtips. On the other hand, beyond feet and footgear, I want leathersex, and leathermen wear boots. What's a toe-sucker to do?

Suck toes. Really, if the guys you want are all wearing boots, and you can't deal with that, one fairly accessible option is to seduce their feet into your mouth bare, or in socks. That, of course, won't get you the wingtips and other foot gear you want.

In *Different Loving* by Gloria Brame (et al), Doug Gaines, the "chief fetishist" of the Foot Fraternity, mentions repeatedly the pleasure he gets from buying shoes for guys, and then putting those shoes on their feet as he takes his pleasure down there in whatever other ways he can get away with. This, or some variant that may involve re-using the same pair for many scenes, might work for you.

A friend of mine, many years ago, found that he couldn't tolerate the standard leatherman outfits people were wearing. Just about all leather clothing, and chaps in particular, looked like "eroti-clown suits" to him. His solution might be adaptable to your situation. He put together a number of outfits—cowboy, business exec, hard hat, etc.—which he found sexier than leather, and made costuming part of the scene when he met someone he wanted to play with. His seduction could be fairly soft because his intent was to get them out of their leathers. He didn't care which costume they chose, how much of it they put on, or whether they bothered with any fantasy scenario to match the costume. So, 99% of the time, he got what he wanted, which was a heavy beating and a lot of verbal abuse without having to bear what he found laughable.

My brain is already boiling over with schemes that would get a leatherman out of his boots and into a pair of selected shoes, and yours must be as well. Consider yourself challenged.

As a bottom, it seems that I don't have a lot to say about conditions in the play scene. For the most part, that's okay, but not when it comes to music. The wrong music (and most of it is way wrong for me) ruins everything. I don't want to be picky or pushy. Is it okay to "force" my music on a Top?

No. It is not okay for a bottom to force his music on a Top any more than it is okay for a Top to force (except when invited to do so) his scene on a bottom. I would seriously consider three solutions if I were you, and I'd come to every scene prepared to implement/accept any of them.

First, get yourself several pairs of good ear plugs. Ask your Tops to let you use them. If you ask in the right submissive mode, you can bring this off.

Second, make a few cassettes of music that works for you. If you're a really good bottom, a really good Top will do whatever he has to do to get the best performance out of you. I suspect this would usually include inspiring you with music of your choice.

Third, tell your Tops you are exceptionally sensitive to the music you hear, and that you need either of the above options in order to give him the service, attention, and extremes you know he is hoping to get from you.

I've heard of SM scenes using food. Except for a cucumber or squash used as a dildo, I can't think how to work food into a scene, but the idea—vague as it is—excites me. Can you give me a hint or two? I don't mind working things out myself, but I don't know where to start.

Scenes involving food are a lot less common in the 90s than they were in the 60s and 70s, now that you mention it. I wonder if this bespeaks a failure of imagination in our hurried times. If so, let's get the creative juices going with a few starting points.

Scenes involving food can be as mundane or as exotic as you choose, as fun or as serious as you want. You can always use foods as sex toys, just as you mention, and go on from there. If a cucumber makes a good ass toy, it will also make a good throat toy. If it works there, peel it and change the sensual experience it gives from hard, cold-surfaced dildo to slimy, organic intrusion. Then chop off a chunk and put it in his mouth as a gag, either telling him he'll be punished for letting it fall out, or helping him out by taping his mouth shut over it. Of course, you have to be careful not to cut a chunk that can *almost* be swallowed for the gag trick. Then, after you played with the cucumber till it's soft, make him eat it, warm and icky as it has become.

Here's another starter: Use a firm banana. Hand it to the bottom, and ask him to show you what he'd like to do to your cock. Of course any course of action can lead to any set of responses you like, from the humorous (and humor is not always out of place in the playroom!) to the highly charged. He can be teased, humiliated, or erotically stimulated as he works, depending on the mood you want to set for the following action. "You'd peel the skin away and bite right through it? Well, no way you're getting at my cock, boy!" No matter what he does with the banana, either it can lead directly to your cock or it can set up a language for the scene in which your cock becomes a goal he may or may not ever attain. And, in the end, the banana (or what remains of it when you stop him) can end up squished on his face, spread on his body, used as lube to fuck him or when he jerks off for you, or it could end up forced into his butt. That ought to get something started.

Yet another general plan is one that I don't feel I need to go into in any detail, but it can be a departure point for lots of different action. Put something edible anywhere on or in your own body, then resist or don't, as you set him the task of getting that food and eating it.

The options, once you get yourself thinking this way, are nearly endless. If a bottom is going to be taking piss anyway, his food might be offered to him floating in a bowl of piss. If he's going to be licking or cleaning the Top's boots, chaps, or other leathers, his food might be given to him smeared on the black leather, in great gobs, or a nibble at a time. Feeding a bottom who is restrained and blindfolded has some interesting dimensions, especially if the Top puts a bit of cleverness into selecting and alternating the foods, or setting up a real-punishment/promised-reward game around the identifying and eating of the foods. See, lots of places to begin, and we didn't even get to scenarios involving dog bowls, eating off the floor, feeding the Top to earn reward points, or torturing the bottom with bizarre foods. This last entry, by the way, was given a good "starter" treatment in the November 1993 issue of *Checkmate*, the SM how-to newsletter.

Nothing so open to variation and re-invention is without risks, of course. There are food reactions and food allergies, diabetes and blood sugar disorders, deeply-seated distastes for certain foods and unexpected associations with others. All of these things can affect the course and safety of a food scene.

Still, food is a fairly safe toy, and bottoms generally know if there are possible problems. And, food play, like most areas of leathersex, improves as the players become more experienced. If nothing else, experience teaches us an increasing variety of ways to intertwine food and play and ways that increase the erotic charge.

Douching is fun, and I do it almost every day, but how can enemas be sexual? Doesn't the shit turn everyone off?

You may slap me for my presumptuousness when next you see me, but your question sounds a bit deceptive to me. In fact, it gives me the feeling that what you really meant to ask is more like, "Where can I find a Top who is into enemas now that I've learned to enjoy the water gushing in and out?" So, the answer in its briefest form is this: No, shit doesn't turn everyone off, some people live for it. There are clubs and pen pal organizations for fans of the flush, lots of personal ads mentioning it, and no shortage of playrooms equipped for it. So? Go for it!

Is it actually possible for a man to stick his whole arm, up to the pit, in another man's ass? Don't the intestines start curving around? And don't they stay in the lower abdomen, anyway, an area shorter than a man's arm?

Yes, the intestines do curve around, but haven't you ever had to reach around the leftovers and the cake to drag a bowl of olives from the back of the bottom shelf of the refrigerator? It's no problem to twist an arm around like a pretzel if you're getting to what you want. And, yes, the bowel is pretty closely confined in the lower abdomen, but have you seen what tight little shapes are described by the arms of a mother holding a newborn infant? Again, no problem, if what you're hugging is important enough to you.

So, yes, it is possible for *some* men to carefully and erotically extend an entire arm inside the asses of *some* other men under just the right conditions, when both of them are in just the right state of mind, and they are properly and intimately connected. This is not a universal possibility. If you cannot do it, whether from Top or bottom, don't fret. If physical depth—getting your arm up there as far as possible—is your entire intention, I wish you no one to play with. Fisting is not a competition sport, and it must not be!

What makes sense to strive for in fisting is the greatest depth of intimacy possible, and the most nearly painless scene you are able to create. If you set out with these goals before you, playing with someone who understands and approves of them, you are likely to also surprise yourself over and over again with the physical outcome of the experience. Meantime, you will be discovering and confirming in yourself a commitment to the less physical side of the scene, which is never a mistake.

For more information and useful details about the inner game of fisting, see Purusha Larkin's *Divine Androgyne*. For excellent coverage of the physical, psychological, and safety aspects of fisting, go to Bert Herrman's *Trust*. Purusha's sole concern (as I understand his book), around which his entire narrative is arranged, is the achievement of ecstasy through esoteric gay male eroticism, including fisting. Herrman's concern is the entire experience of fisting, which he calls handballing. Besides discussing safe ways to achieve depth of penetration, the author wisely describes other pleasures and safety issues, and touches on a variety of spiritual interpretations of the intense experience of handballing.

6

GOING TO EXTREMES

It is important to remember as you look at these questions about extreme scenes that there is no reason to think everyone who is doing leathersex will eventually require more and more extreme stimulation. The level of intensity a person wants is not necessarily progressive at all. Extreme scenes are the province of players who want to or must play at such levels, and these people often know before their first experience that they want or need something of unusual intensity.

I really get turned on only when I doubt my safety, even fear for my life. I don't mind real risk, but I never even get a believable simulation. What to do?

This question, which is related to queries about scary scenes versus ones that are negotiated under the safe-sane-consensual credo, becomes somewhat surprising when I notice that my correspondent this time is a man who has been playing hard for 10 years or more. It isn't that time in the scene necessarily means a man already knows it all. On the contrary, the longer I am in the scene, the more new questions and concerns I run into. Also, a question can suddenly crop up when a player loses a longtime partner or circle of buddies.

It's not easy for a long-experienced player to have to deal with a question as basic as this one, but time marches on, delivering us into novel situations along the way.

The best answer I can come up with for this man is this: Find one or more sadistic Tops who are acceptable to you as trustworthy and reliable partners, and give them a *carte blanche* to take their sadistic pleasure any way they want to. With careful and thorough cruising and networking, you can find candidates who will be as glad to find you as you are to find them.

I don't know exactly how you might be able to use it, but I can suggest that you look into the Metropolitan Slave Correctional Institute in Chicago. The dean of the MsCI and publisher of *Metropolitan Slave Magazine*, jeb, seems to understand the kind of scenes you want, even if his accent on slavery as a permanent condition may not help the two of you to connect profitably. There have been other training centers around the country over the years as well. With a careful search of current resources, you can find a few at any given time. And, much as I might not like to suggest commercial enterprises for leathersex purposes, they do provide an option that can blossom, one way or another, into more acceptable solutions.

Something from the next Q&A might also be useful in pursuing a final answer to this question.

I try, both as a Top and a bottom, to do things as hot and extreme as the stories in *Drummer* and *Manifest Reader*, but it all seems impossible when you get right down to it. Is it? Don't the people who publish this material try to give us some kind of instructive or useful information in the magazines?

Going To Extremes

I have never doubted that creative SM men can do things *hotter* than anything a writer can put into a story. On the other hand, to be as hot as the fictions in magazines, or hotter, does not mean that reality *follows* the guidelines deduced from short stories. Not at all!

More specifically, it should be understood by all readers that the stories in most magazines are not meant to be realistic, and they often include a great deal of action that would be either unsafe or impossible. Notices to this effect are often published among the boilerplate statements in magazines. Even magazines like *Bound & Gagged*, filled with "true" experiences described in letters and stories from readers, may also be filled with either exaggerations or fantasies the writers believe are realistic.

If you want useful information about doing safe scenes, you need to look into the expressly indicated nonfiction columns in the magazines that carry such commentary. There are also publications dedicated to nothing but delivering the real facts about leathersex and fetish activity. *Checkmate/DungeonMaster* come to mind, as do the newsletters of a lot of leather/SM clubs.

Fiction is also useful information, of course, even if it describes action that cannot be duplicated. Inspiration has value, for one thing. Besides, some of the most impossible scenes ever written and published are great fantasies, and they can be enacted in the same sense that we can have angels or superman or leprechauns in stage shows. With a clever blend of sensual stimulations and verbal (over)statements along with a mutually accepted pact to play out a given story, something very hot can be evolved. It may be better to choose the essential element from a piece of fiction (or elements from several), and leave the actual course of the fantasy to the imagination of the Top. This will work better for most bottoms since it means they can still be surprised and frightened.

I've read about the Sun Dance done by Native Americans, and Fakir Musafar's modern version, as well as the ball dances, the "O-Kee-Pa" and similar cultural rites that involve some sort of possible pain. I wonder, though, is any of it SM?

You decide. It is SM, in my view, if the people doing it choose to apply that label. By my own more personal definition, no stimulation a man provides and controls for himself is properly called SM. This is just about labeling, though, and doesn't imply any judgement of any kind. I have used beds of nails and done ball dances, I have assisted at a Sun Dance and helped a woman into a Hindu-ritual kavadi frame. While I wouldn't call any of these things SM or leathersex, I understand that they were (in the cases I mentioned) being done by SM players and leatherfolk for reasons that shared something important with their sexual inclination to pain-related stimulation.

Choosing to be hard-nosed about definitions in any but the most private circles usually leads to disastrous misunderstandings. Ease up. Do what makes you feel good, and call it SM if that makes your approach to it more acceptable to you. Or call it athleticism or yoga if you prefer. Making convincing arguments for applying any of these labels to the activities mentioned in the question would be pretty easy.

I've seen Stellarc (just in books) and I want to hang by piercings the way he does, but I don't know what's possible and not, how to do what can be done, where to learn what I have to learn. Is there a single source, or is this something to be learned only by trial and dangerous error?

No and no. There is no single source of instructional information for doing body suspensions like the ones for which Stellarc is famous. There is no reason to think that "trial and *dangerous* error" is the only alternative. There are a few people besides Stellarc who seem to be well-informed about this, among them Fakir Musafar in the San Francisco Bay Area, and a properly approached relationship with anyone who seriously shares such an esoteric interest might represent major steps towards your goal.

The way to go about it without an expert at hand is still not "trial and dangerous error." As with any extreme scene, it is always possible for two or several interested people to get together to work out what is required. You can do this in carefully planned steps, reworking your plan after each experiment.

You might try working out what equipment you need. Be logical. You can multiply the test strength of a cord or wire times the number of cords you intend to use to see what their total lifting strength is. Or, you can divide the weight to be suspended by the test strength of the cord to determine what is the *absolute* minimum number of cords to be used. You can guess that the hooks—fish hooks, for example—must be barbless to be used in this way. You will either be able to find barbless hooks or polish away the barbs on available hooks. You may need to learn how the knots are tied in fishing line. You may have to do some research on the pulley and other equipment to be used. And, at some point, you will want to start testing everything as you learn to do what you will eventually be doing.

Do you think you should do a test suspension with many times more cords than you believe are necessary, and with the cords looped under body parts rather than hooked into the flesh? Do you want to do further dry runs with just the hooks, more or less doing piercing scenes in preparation for the upcoming suspension? Would you like to try suspending one or both legs, or maybe all four limbs, while leaving the bulk of the body weight resting on a table or bed? I'd think these were all good ideas.

You will want to plan very carefully the method by which you may finally take the step from suspended body parts to full suspension. Some of the famous Stellarc suspensions involved boulders as counterweights and huge teams of helpers. Simpler suspensions, not necessarily involving flesh hooks, often make use of a table or bed that can be lowered at the appropriate moment. Since an inch is much the same as a mile of space beneath a suspended body, another method I've seen used is interesting: An inflated air mattress under the body can be deflated when all the hooks and cords are in place.

Think seriously about how long you will remain suspended. Often, only seconds are tolerable. And, obviously, think about how the suspension will be ended, both in case of success and in case of emergency.

A dedicated person might very well spend a year or so developing the skills and gathering the equipment for such a scene. Then you might want to do your first full flesh-hook suspension as a very private affair, or share it with an audience. You might want it to be a video affair or a photo opportunity. Think carefully about what will heighten the overall experience for yourself, and work steadily toward that, avoiding *dangerous* errors by constant vigilance and careful progress.

When you do breath control, how do you know when to let the bottom breathe again? I don't want to wimp out, so I need to discover when you HAVE to let them breathe.

I can't give you any exact instructions about breath control. It's not that I don't do such scenes. I do, but anything anyone can say could be dangerous for anyone else to try to do.

Learning breath control technique by bottoming to experienced Tops doesn't result in the development of complete confidence either. The difference between the inner experience of the bottom and that of the Top in this scene is more profound than in most other kinds of play. The answer, if there is *one* answer, has to be a combination of all the usually effective tactics for building SM skills, but with all of them given more serious and careful attention. Bottoming to a good Top, discussing the experience with the same Top and with other players (Top and bottom), practicing the technique in a cautiously progressive way, reading whatever may be written on the subject, and observing your own scenes with intense attention are all ways to work on this skill. Then, as your confidence grows—almost always lagging somewhat behind your actual skill level—you will become able to perform more and more complete scenes with constantly increasing effects and safety.

If you suspect for a moment that your confidence is not building logically, that it is not lagging reasonably behind your skill level, stop. You're dangerous.

Can ball-beating result in permanent change, like larger balls? And is there any danger of permanent damage?

Hmmm? You leave me wondering about what you may mean by "damage" if you are so prepared to welcome permanently enlarged testicles. There is, of course, always a danger of permanent damage of a sort that no one would be able to welcome when any body part is beaten. Balls are much less fragile than novice torturers and their victims might think, but much more easily injured than most other body parts. All you have to do in order to get a fairly clear picture of the extreme possibilities is watch one or two of the videos produced and distributed by the Ball Club.

One of the Ball Club's tapes, however, carries four full screens of warnings. For your edification, I reproduce them below, but for a great deal more edification, take a look at the tapes.

Warning!! Warning!! Warning!!

This videotape was made by actors who are very experienced devotees of a conduct in which they engage, and which is depicted on this tape. The acts in this video should not be imitated by members of the general public and should be left to those who are familiar with them. Engaging in this conduct by inexperienced persons could result in severe pain and potentially permanent injury.

The actors depicted in this videotape are stuntmen who have unusually insensitive testicles and scrota, and have developed this physiologically unusual quality, with which they were born, by careful study and practice. They know what to do, what not to do and, most of all, what their own limits are. Do not do what you see on the videotape unless you are knowledgeable and experienced in it.

The following videotape is being presented as a visual fantasy, and it has been prepared and intended solely for viewing by a special and limited audience, namely adults over 21 years of age, who request and desire viewing of sexually explicit material for the purpose of information, education, and entertainment in the privacy of their own home.

This video fantasy may not be sold or exhibited to any minor nor to any person[s] who do not wish to view it, except consenting adults who agree to view the film. All actors are 18 years of age or older. Proof of ages is on file.

Safe sex is for everyone. Do not allow alcohol or drugs to impair your judgement.

There you have the concern of the "pros" about the possibility of permanent damage, but you also have the basic instructions for becoming a pro: study and practice carefully and much.

I really do want to be castrated. Used to be I wanted a super-Master to nut me and keep me for life. Now, I'd accept less Mastering to get real surgery. Is it possible? What will happen from having my nuts removed? Not much, I think, since I am already nearly 50.

My usually-reliable medical consultant has refused to comment on this one. He says there is far too little "adequately interpreted" information available on the subject of mid-life castration for him or anyone to make definitive statements on the subject. He hints that there may be important roles for sex hormones to play at all stages of human life, roles which he is sure are not yet understood.

Another, no less reliable but slightly more adventurous commentator tells me that you should expect, even at your age, some of the same effects a younger man would experience from the loss of his balls. That is, a general alteration in all hormone-related sex characteristics such as muscle bulk, how your body stores fat, whisker and hair growth, and so forth. He adds that he imagines anyone actually eager to be castrated could probably tolerate the effects, especially if they were predicted relatively accurately. On the other hand, being a trained nurse, he leans toward encouraging you to find a surgeon willing to perform the operation under standard, modern, hospital conditions. It seems medico #2 is more concerned with the risk of infection than the problems that may accrue due to lack of male hormones.

My own feeling is that unless you have a cooperative surgeon who is a Top and as hungry for this scene as you are, you ought not to think of being castrated in play space or even in a leathersex frame of mind. Remember, too, that even an eager surgeon who is a Top may feel ethically constrained. So, you may be able to arrange a castration in a hospital—a private hospital, at an exorbitant rate—in the U.S. or overseas, but the sexual value of the event will have to be in its contemplation and display rather than its execution.

I've seen photos of a saline-inflated scrotum. I want to see my sac stretched out like that. Can I do it myself? Using what kind of materials? Do I need instructions, and does anyone sell such instructions?

You can inflate your own scrotum, although there is a slight chance that you will faint in the process or experience an illogical and confusing panic. With these possible eventualities in mind, I'd advise against doing your own inflation the first time, at least. The instructions are fairly simple actually, and I suppose they could even be spelled out here, but I am not a nurse or doctor, and I may not know all the potential problems that you should be aware of, or all the questions I should have you answer before proceeding.

About once a year, QSM in San Francisco offers a class and demonstration, and such scenes also take place at Inferno where experienced Tops are not in short supply. Also, if you delve into your personal network a bit, you may find that you know an experienced person with access to the supplies. Failing that, poke around a little more widely for the address of a supply house that can provide your necessities and instructions. Since I am uncertain of the legality of selling angiocaths and saline solution without prescriptions in your area, I feel more than a little nervous about giving an address in a book.

All of this points up an important fact about extreme scenes: If you really want a particular kind of action, you sometimes have to put a lot of time, energy, money, and ego risk into the research and preparation. A scrotal inflation is worth it, believe me, and you should have a photographer on hand to extend the experience over the years for you.

Can tits be enlarged in "real time" or does it actually take years and years as I have heard?

Tits can be temporarily enlarged, as I'm sure you know, very quickly. Have you partner suck them hard for a few minutes, or put a snake bite cup over each nipple for 10 or 20 minutes, or just pull each nipple out and tie it off with a length of thick string. Voila! Instant nipple enlargement.

Of course, I know this is hardly what you had in mind, but it is what can be done quickly, and it is not pointless. With the blood stockpiled in your nipples and the skin stretched over it, you'll find them hypersensitive and easily pleasured.

More lasting enlargement takes more time to achieve, but that should not be a problem since we are talking about intense play, not long, boring sessions of hard labor. If the only kind of tit work you get (or give yourself) is the sensitizing sort mentioned in the previous paragraph, you'll have to do it very often and very long each time to ever see a significant change in the dimensions of your nipples. What works best and lasts longest is deeper and harder work. I am told that at least one reason nipples grow larger with crushing and twisting and biting is that they are eventually damaged inside enough to produce scar tissue. This might even be true, and I have some evidence to support it in the fact that just *one* of my tits was worked really hard for a number of years, and it was very hard to get a piercing needle through it years later.

I am told by a friend with impressive nipples that he worked at getting the measurements he now has for only about seven years. His method was to date only men who were going to abuse his tits, then do everything he could to get them to challenge their own limits by working on his tits as they had never attacked any before. He prepared for these dates by pumping his nipples up and tying them off *every day*. He says there was a noticeable and pleasing change in apparently permanent size within six to eight months, and that his nipples were big enough to attract comments—both jealous and disgusted—in no more than 18 months. Is that real time? Well, anyway, that's real information.

I have the supplies and I've read the instructions in a couple of magazine articles (like your own "Edge Play" article in *Drummer*, Sir), but I'm still nervous about playing with fire. Can you tell me how to get over it and get on with it?

First, let's be clear, you did not read instruction for playing with fire in my "Edge Play" article (*Drummer* #148, April, 1991). I intentionally edited my remarks on every subject in that article in order not to give anyone the impression that, by reading it, they should be informed enough to undertake the action. I've done the same thing in every similar article I have ever written about extreme scenes.

If you have read enough instruction to actually own supplies that are precisely what you need, all that remains is to approach the scene with respect for the fire's capacity to destroy, and a clear understanding that you cannot have learned the most important things about fire play from reading articles. Long and careful experimentation is the only possible substitute for learning from an experienced player.

One way to experiment carefully and with a relatively high safety level is to perform your first fire scenes on yourself while you are standing in a bathtub full of water. Do not do your experiment on a body part that requires you to look down in order to perform or watch the few seconds of flaming play. An outstretched arm, for instance, is much better than your belly or thigh. Follow your instructions exactly, and comfort yourself with the fact that you can drop into the water fairly safely if you must.

Beyond that, I am still unwilling to give instructions. Maybe you understand.

Is necrophilia—or the fantasy simulation of it—leathersex? If so, do you think a person who has such fantasies should find a way to act on them or should he seek psychological help to forget it?

This is a very difficult question. I don't like to say "Don't." And, I don't want to encourage anyone to do anything I have never done and would not consider doing. Yes, there is a judgement implied, but I can get over myself better than that.

Necrophilic sex does happen. It happens more often than anyone wants to know, but it can almost never be leathersex by my definition since the dead man is in no position to consent or resist, not to mention the fact that it can hardly be legal.

The fantasy of having sex with a dead person is actually

understandable, though. If what you want is to carry the resignation of will or the assumption of power to its absolute limits, there could be no more perfectly expressive scene than necrophilia. Performed in fantasy by consenting adults, this kind of sex can be very telling—exposing to yourself more than to anyone else the roots and branches of your urge to dominate or submit.

There's is really no need to get into either the ways that real necrophilia happens or the ways to compose a fantasy scene on the subject. The former is a taboo I am unwilling to deal with here (perhaps the only one). The latter is easy enough to work out for yourself.

Then, your question: Should you find ways to act on your urge or get professional help? My advice, which you should consider carefully before making your own decision, is that you should, first, find one or more partners with whom to play out the scene. Then, secondly, if you feel the need to continue onward from fantasy scenes to contact with an actual corpse, seek help. I don't know that I have an actual moral problem with the concept of necrophilia, but I do have a problem with the potential complications—dragging others into your scene unwanted, risking jail or prison, and risking disease as well. What's more, I know that this kind of desire tends to be self-destructive. If that is a difficult statement for you to understand, consider this: Sex ought to be about life, not just *choosing* life as the Christians say, but *making* life—constantly creating and recreating life, intensifying it and making it more attractive—as every cell in your body knows.

Anything that subverts the preference for life over death is suspect, perhaps even inherently dangerous to the human spirit.

I have always been fascinated by the concept of branding, and have enjoyed fictions (I think they are) with brandings of cowboy bottoms in them. Now I have heard that branding of humans really can and does happen. So, it's safe, right? Where do I get the branding irons and things? Can I use the same

irons that I see (and have already collected a few of) that used to be used on cows?

No, you may not use your collection of brands made for cattle on humans. The effect would be infection and gangrene, and not a brand. All the same, branding of humans can and does happen. There are even commercial body modification studios where brandings are done by appointment. While there may not be businesses doing branding in your area, the fact remains that body modification studios are a good place to start any search for a brand. In most areas, the businesses you are looking for (as a starting point) are piercing shops. Very few piercers do brands, but it would be hard for a piercer not to know if anyone were doing branding in the neighborhood.

Since I know several people who proudly sport brands, and a few who had brands done only to have them grow invisible over a relatively short period of years, I feel comfortable saying that brands done by knowledgeable practitioners can be completely safe. I have never seen a botched brand, but I've heard of one. It was done under outdoor scene conditions. It was the first brand attempted by the Top. It was not something the bottom wanted by any means. And—surprise—it never healed properly, and eventually involved a four-square-inch skin graft.

Be careful, and invite me to the ritual that includes your first brand.

Everyone seems excited about cuttings and scarifications, sort of replacing tattoos in a way. I have two questions about this: First, is it easier to work cuttings and scar-making into real scenes? Second, what's going wrong with the cuttings my friend has gotten—they have just healed and disappeared.

Cuttings and scarifications do seem to be increasingly popular these days, adding to the options for those who want to do permanent body modifications. As for working cuttings into a scene, I'd say that, yes, it is easier to construct a *sense* of scene around cutting than around tattooing, or to approach cutting with a scene-based attitude. This is not the same thing as working cutting into a scene. It still seems to me that for hygienic reasons as well as reasons connected to more general safety questions, it is better not to think of cutting as something you might insert into a scene. What's more, the idea of working a cutting into a scene presupposes that the Top in the scene is trained and skilled in cuttings, and few actually are. To do a cutting properly requires more preparation than just watching someone else do it, you know, and far more than just seeing a few finished cuttings.

If you have access to a Top who wants to do a cutting on your body and you want to have that cutting done by that person on that body part right now, go for it *so long as you are convinced he knows what to do and how to handle any emergency that may come up*. The other way to get a scene-cutting combination would be to arrange to have the experienced and trusted cutter come in to your play space to do a cutting during a scene between you and your playmate(s). In this case, I'd like to know that the players were at least generally aware of the needs of the cutter and how to treat the cutting after it has been done.

As for the cuttings that grow away: Different people respond differently to cuts—whether intentional and decorative or accidental—and most of us know how easily we scar or how completely we heal without scarring. The expertise of the cutter can make a difference as well, but supposing the cutting was done deeply enough to scar, the scarring tendencies and general health of the body being cut are the primary factors in predicting the need to repeat the cutting process. Also, if a person treats a cutting very, very nicely, as he might treat an accidental cut, soothing it with emollients and washing it gently, he is undermining the scarring process. Some cutters will disagree with me on this one, but I suggest that beyond avoiding infection, you should treat a cutting roughly. Pick or scrub the scabs off early, leave the area dry and exposed to air as much as possible, and don't baby it. Even with rough treatment, cuttings often need to be done more than once, sometimes several times, to build up a visible scar.

Of course, the best cutters will frequently work pigments or other materials into the fresh cutting. These can help by irritating the cut into less "perfect" healing, and they can retain the visibility of the cutting even if the scarring is very slight.

I've had some beautiful whippings that left my back opened up and bleeding, but I don't scar. I want to have "battle scars," but I guess I can't have them. That is, I can't unless you have some suggestions that will move me from hopelessly flawless to gloriously scarred.

Allow me to pass to you the advice of Peter Fiske, one of the most "gloriously scarred" of all whipping bottoms: "Pick the scabs!" The answer above about cuttings may hold some interest for you, but repeating a whip mark exactly would be difficult, and working in pigments might be a little silly (or, would it?), but you can at least pick the scabs, which will encourage scarring especially if the cuts are fairly deep.

7

SORTING OUT RELATIONSHIPS

In the questions I have collected here, the problems with sorting out relationships are often more about labels or words than actions. Popular wisdom tells us the word is not the thing as the map is not the territory. Nonetheless, words can be powerful, particularly when they define how we feel about ourselves and each other.

How much should a bottom, boy, or slave give up for a Top? Does your answer change if I define myself by one or another of these different terms? I can't say which word will apply when I do get into a relationship, that depends on the other man and our connection. And it should, shouldn't it?

How much should anyone give up for anyone? The answer, in my view, is only what can be given freely. This usually means we give up little we are not eager to be free of and that, if we give up more, it is going to hurt. And that leaves you to deal with the question of how much of the hurtful giving you are willing to bear. The healthy answer to that usually revolves around compromises or trade-offs. If you're getting something you really want and won't easily find elsewhere, you may be willing to give up a bit more of something you had intended not to relinquish.

If a relationship calls for you to give up something you value and gives you nothing of *greater* value in exchange, the sense of loss or resentment is likely to sour the possibilities otherwise inherent in the coupling. Weighing such trade-offs can be tricky, and generally you'd be wise to err on the side of self-preservation rather than push yourself to accommodate a loss or limitation you don't find acceptable.

The words with which we label ourselves and our partners do represent something about the superficial equalities and inequities (of roles, at least) in our relationships, but it is people not words we want to be concerned with. Words like Master and slave, Man/Daddy and boy, Top and bottom, lover, significant other, and property should be called on only to describe our relationships. The words are conveniences, not prescriptions. A self-identified boy may be saying he's willing to give up less of his liberty and self-determination than is the case with another man who chooses to identify himself as a slave. Still, either person may find himself comfortable *in a particular relationship* with either term, as long as the actual workings of the relationship are comfortable, exciting, and fulfilling.

Words must be bent to conform to human lives. People must not sculpt their lives to facilitate labels.

I am supposed to be a slave, but my Master doesn't give me enough to do to keep busy. Do you think I'm failing to take steps to keep myself busy, or is he failing to use me fully, or is sexual slavery just that much like being a 1950s housewife?

To be a slave is largely to be committed to the comfort, convenience, and satisfaction of another man. If you are doing all he asks of you, and he is pleased with your performance, you are faced with the constant challenge of making his life more comfortable, convenient, and satisfying by the application of your own wits and skills, and the use of your apparently free time. A slave who stops functioning because he has been given no specific orders, or because he has checked off everything on his task list, becomes a burden rather than a convenience pretty quickly.

You might check with your Master. Maybe he'd like to give you more to do, but believes you are doing all you are capable of already. If you have additional time and energy available, try saying something like this: "Sir, I am pleased to serve and be used as you will, and I feel I have a responsibility to report that I have more time and energy than you are using at this time. If you do not have more demands to make of me, I would like your permission to pursue my own ideas about what I can do to serve you better. Sir, what would you have me do?"

Your Master's response will set your direction, whether he gives you new responsibilities or sets you to work on your own plans. Or, for that matter, he may say that what he wants you to do with your extra time is stand still in such and such a place, watch certain TV shows, or whatever. Just remember not to replace his plans for you with your own. What you invent for yourself to do should complement and extend your Master's use of you and your services, not subvert or supplant his intentions.

What do I do if my Master orders me to do something my conscience says is wrong? He's not ordering murder, but what he wants might be illegal.

The question of whether to follow a Master's orders can only have one answer: If you are the slave and you are committed to doing your Master's bidding, then you must *always* do as you are told. If your relationship permits you to question orders, do so only when you must, but proceed with caution.

If, in the end, you find you must refuse your Master, then you must get out of the relationship. The egos and emotions of men in any kind of relationship can be very fragile, but the more demanding the relationship, the more its basic tenets are absolute. The Master-slave relationship affords some intense and magnificent physical, emotional, and spiritual opportunities to both partners if, and only if, the predetermined foundation of the relationship can be maintained unchallenged.

I suggest that all potential Master-slave couples "live in sin" for a few months before outlining the details of their expectations in a written or even a verbal contract. This provides the possibility that each man will discover how the other operates, reducing the fear of surprises, like the one that inspired this question.

Specifically about doing something that might be illegal, my first thought is that we have to be careful about laws. We can't go about breaking laws without considering the possible consequences. Neither can we panic about breaking laws which, if followed, will destroy our lives. It may be, for example, that the states criminalizing sodomy do so hoping that all gays will move elsewhere, but are we willing to give up home, family, career, and familiar surroundings—or, alternatively, sex!—to avoid breaking a law? I don't think so.

If your Master is asking you to break a law you feel morally compelled to obey, think carefully before you act. You may want to live with your Master, even live *for* your Master, but you must always live with yourself.

I think of myself as a slave in search of a Master, but I still resent being told what to do. Do I need an attitude adjustment, a change of identity, or what?

Who knows what will work for you? No one, if not yourself.

Do you really want to find a Master, a man who will take responsibility for and control of your life? Or, is it that you just want to be free of responsibility for yourself without accepting anyone else's "say" in your life? That's for you to think about, and you might want to include in your thinking the first question and answer of this chapter.

Now, let me share with you a piece of personal history you may find useful. When I came out into leathersex, bottoms—especially novice bottoms—were under pretty severe restrictions in the circles I knew. We didn't speak unless we were both spoken to and also given permission to respond. We wore no clothing in the presence of Tops and moved immediately to comply with the orders of any Top present. We had no names, and were given none. We never looked at a Top above the knees except on specific orders to do so, nor ever touched a Top at all except when told to. And there was a lot more to it even than that. It was inevitable that I would resist and resent a lot of it, but somewhere in my heart—the part of myself I trust most—I felt a compulsion to accept the restrictions, to express little resistance, and to vent no resentment. Moreover, I took my punishment without complaint when any Top noticed my little shows of resistance, which were seldom more than fleeting facial expressions.

Why did I put up with all of this? Not because I felt powerless, but because the simplicity and clarity of the situation helped me feel powerful enough to bear absolutely anything. In that circle, I felt that I was totally safe, fully protected, strongly supported, and—although such terminology would never have been tolerated—I felt respected. I was taught to be sure enough of my indissoluble individuality that I could perform as a nameless and apparently will-less appliance. I admit that I felt an urge to reject the limiting conditions placed on me, but I *chose* instead to go with the program, and ended up satisfying some very deep longings in the process. Along the way, I also learned exactly what the power exchange is and how beautiful it can be when it works.

In short, I was giving my truest and most urgent feelings and needs power over my fantastic self-image and my untested sense of worth, by constantly choosing to submit to others. I've never regretted the choice.

Is shaving the *sine qua non* of erotic slavery? Is a shaved head always required of a serious slave? I don't think I can do that, or let that be done, but I want the rest of what I imagine is involved in slavery.

The shaving of slaves has a long, long history. I am told the Romans shaved the bodies of slaves sent to serve the gladiators, and I feel no need to research this legend. I like accepting it as true. Nonetheless, I also know of Masters who like hair on their slaves, which is more than enough justification for a slave to remain unshaven.

Shaving, as often as not, is done to reduce the appearance of manhood in the slave (or symbolize that idea), and to emphasize the masculinity of the Master by comparison. Submitting to a complete shaving, particularly for a slave who treasures his hair, can be an experience or symbol of total submission to another man. And still, the option to shave a slave or not is open to be decided in every new relationship. There is no visible *sine qua non* of modern erotic slavery.

One possible solution for a Master and slave who cannot both be comfortable with either permanent hairlessness or continued furriness would be an annual shaving. I know of one long term relationship in which this anniversary ritual worked well. Another would be shaving all body parts normally covered by the slave's usual work or outdoor clothing. And I've known a number of Masters who have been satisfied to leave their slaves' body hair alone, sometimes demanding a shaved crotch, clearings around the nipples, deforestation of the ass crack, or whatever.

Of course, these days, Masters with no policy on hair or

shaving are pretty common too.

Do M/s relationships require a) living together, b) contracts, c) slave chastity and Master liberty?

Briefly, Master-slave relationships, by definition, require what the Master requires. So, none of the things you mention are essential, but if the Master requires any of them any slave who submits to him is accepting the requirements he outlines.

Is a slave necessarily a bimbo? I've tried slaves, three of them, and they're all alike. They're windup toys that come to a stop if I stop winding them. Am I beating my head against an immovable object, or is it possible to find a slave with a mind?

I have no doubt at all that my last slave, warren, was one of the most intelligent people I've ever known. He was a skilled chemist (biochemical spectrography), a computer whiz, and a remarkable slave who always seemed to know by the time I did, often sooner, what would please me. He organized his time in such a way that his chores were done well and fully, leaving him time to go to the gym, romp with the dog, maintain close family ties, and get all the rest he needed at no cost to me in terms of comfort, convenience, or satisfaction.

Bozos, bimbos, idiots, and sloths turn up often, wanting to be slaves, but they have nothing to exchange for the guidance, safety, liberty, and pleasure a good Master provides.

A good slave is hard to find. I was just phenomenally lucky to have a friend find warren and send him my way when I had been slaveless for several months. More often, a Master has to take a physically interesting, sufficiently intelligent, and genuinely motivated boy and teach him how to perform as required. Such training is, of course, wasted on bimbos and their ilk.

In a Master-slave relationship, things can get confusing. Who should drive the car? Who should keep the checkbook? Who should write the shopping list and decide what's for dinner?

There are no shoulds and no rules about these things for Master-slave relationships or, for that matter, any relationships. I find it convenient to have my slave do the driving, keep track of the money and pay the bills, provide my meals based on what he knows of my preferences, and otherwise attend to the details of the household without much discussion. Other Masters feel better if they must give orders constantly and if they reserve to themselves whatever elements of housekeeping they see as issues of control, very often including both the checkbook and the car keys.

Far from being confusing, all such questions are answered by the basis of the relationship. That is, in the opinion of the Master, what can this slave do that will contribute to the Master's comfort, convenience, and satisfaction. Once that is determined, everything else falls into place.

How do you feel about "Property of . . ." tattoos or other permanent signs of relationships?

My feeling is that marks of ownership, even permanent markings that are very specific about any relationship, should be applied later rather than earlier, and they should be such that the marked man believes he will be glad to bear them for life. Masters die. Lovers grow apart. Slaves become Masters. Relationships disintegrate. And, like it or not, fashions in body marking and modification change. All of these factors should be considered in deciding to mark one or both partners in a relationship.

My last two slaves—scott and warren—were both tattooed for me. Scott designed and begged for a tattoo in which my astrological sign dominated his. Warren, who was uncomfortable wearing his chain collar around his mother, accepted a barbed wire "collar" tattooed so it was completely covered by any shirt he'd wear around his family. Both the zodiacal design and the barbed wire (matching my tattooed barbed wire harness) were personal for us and fully represented ownership. Both could also have been worn beyond the confines of our relationships if the boys had survived, and we had separated.

I don't disapprove of tattoos that announce the wearer is the slave and/or property of another man, but I have seen slaves wearing bizarre markings which are actually covers tattooed over no longer accurate property markings.

If I really love my boy, I ought to do anything to satisfy and please him, shouldn't I? But I can't. He wants me to suck his cock. He wants to come every day. He wants days off from Daddy, meaning, days off from me, from our relationship. What would you do to correct, punish, or ???? such a boy?

If you really love anyone, what you want most is that person's happiness. Does that mean you have to suck his cock, that he has to be helped to an orgasm every day, that he can independently demand an open relationship that allows him outside sexual opportunities? No, it doesn't. What it does mean is that if you can't negotiate solutions to these problems without curtailing the boy's happiness, the most loving solution will be to end the relationship. Think carefully and work hard at other options before you choose to separate, but it seems to me never worthwhile to save a relationship that guarantees unhappiness for either or both parties.

There is a hint in your question that you were expecting slavish compliance to your will from a man who is identified as your boy. Usually, boys are not slaves. They have neither made the extreme commitment to another man that is expected of a slave nor are they demanding the corresponding degree of commitment from their partner.

A boy may want and accept guidance from his Daddy, but he

is in “slave mode” if he hops up to follow Daddy's orders without questioning them. This is not necessarily a problem, of course, and many couples swing around freely on the clock-face of possible terms and conditions for relationships.

I really don't want to put too fine a point on the definition of a boy. As I've said above, the words are there for our convenience, but we want to use them in ways that both partners in a relationship understand similarly. A boy is usually understood to be growing toward manhood, with Daddy's guidance and help; while a slave is attempting to form himself into not his own man, but the best answer he can be to his Master's needs.

You say that your boy wants to come every day. Yes, and why shouldn't a boy come as often as he likes? A slave, on the other hand, might be expected to come only with the permission of his Master.

Living with a boy can be delicious, but the boundaries in all directions need to be made very clear. If one partner more than the other tends toward a lover-to-lover or Master-to-slave relationship, course corrections may be required to restore the apparently expected Daddy-to-boy dynamic.

Daddy has always been Daddy to me. Now he wants me to fuck him. How can I do that? He's Dad, isn't he?

Assuming that Dad's ass isn't too ugly to be fucked, and assuming that you love Dad and want him to be happy, there's no reason in the world why you shouldn't plug his butt. Fucking is lovemaking, isn't it? Does it matter so much who is sticking into whom? No, it doesn't! Feel as good about yourself as you can, boy, and do for Daddy whatever you can that makes him happy. The only reason I can imagine for trying to get out of fucking Dad when he wants it is that you might not *like* to do that, meaning it might get in the way of your own happiness. If so, explain that to him. If not, enjoy the comfort of having a fuck buddy at home.

A friend of mine read your question, and wrote this note in the margin: "I like to think of it as serving Daddy any way I can. As long as I understand that, and keep my understanding of it, I don't lose my moorings."

I am older than my Dad, and that didn't bother me when we were getting together, but now it keeps running into embarrassing problems at parties and other social situations. It's almost got me ready to give up on the relationship. Do you have a less drastic solution?

Any relationship that surprises people can cause embarrassing situations and become publicly complicated, but there are always ways to reduce the surprise factor. Meantime, understand that anything you do to make public situations easier for yourselves will also smooth the way for other couples like yourselves.

My idea may sound silly, but I'd try it if I were in your boots. Get two brass badges engraved. One says, "Older BOY of a younger Dad." The other, "Younger DAD of an older boy." Make it very easy for the men around you to grasp your view of your relationship *quickly* and, if they're worthy of their leathers, they'll accept and celebrate the arrangement.

Absolutely don't let outside pressures about how you run your relationship cause you a problem. Outsiders are . . . well, they're outsiders, and they don't get to vote on your pleasures.

My lover and I have never had a problem with the word lover, but we've learned to appreciate calling ourselves "partners" which seems to sit better with our leather friends. Now, it seems, we are experiencing some pressure to sort ourselves out under more descriptive leathersex labels, and we're uncomfortable. He makes most of the decisions, so I suppose I could think of him as Dad, and I'd be okay with "boy." I do all the errands and housework—gladly so—but neither of us think Master and

slave works. Really, what we want is the labeling that gets us out of the label game. What do you recommend?

I suggest you stick to your own comfortable choice. You might even try the idea I suggested to the couple in the previous question and answer, although it seems a less than perfect solution for you. Still, the idea would be badges saying, "Robert's Partner" and "Bill's Partner." They'd be interesting conversation pieces at least.

In the end, you are what you are to each other, and the labels matter very little. I know the leather community in your city is small—everyone knows everyone, or so it seems. That being the case, if you're tired of pushing folks to leave you alone as *partners* and you want to appease rather than instruct, it wouldn't hurt to play along. Call Bill "Dad" in public, ask him to call you "boy" if he's okay with that. It shouldn't matter at all, but in some close-knit communities harmless compliance is smoother than harmless non-compliance.

As for getting yourselves out of the labeling game, choosing labels that others accept will do that. Choosing to use Dad and boy does it better than most other options too, since no two Dad-boy couples are much alike. This means that *all* you buy into with Dad and boy is the label. While Master and slave are labels that bear some pretty detailed expectations (many of which are privately ignored by any given couple), people don't have a terribly specific idea of how Dads and boys should or do relate to one another. If, for example, Daddy-Bill goes to the bar and brings back a drink for boy-Robert, it won't cause a raised eyebrow, much less the consternation that would ensue if a self-declared Master carried a drink to his slave.

In fact, accepting Dad and boy means—if you so choose—you go on as partners, nothing changes except that everyone leaves you alone *on this one subject*.

If I agree to be a man's dog, will I be kept on a leash, on my knees, in dog mode all the time?

If you agree to be a man's dog, you will surely find out what you mean and what he means by "dog" before you finalize that agreement. In the rare cases of relationships in which one partner becomes a dog for more than a few hours, the role has been very extreme. The dog doesn't speak, takes whatever treatment it gets, eats what it is fed, etc. Of course, a man cannot expect much more than barking from a full-time dog while he is away. Dirty plates and pans tempt a dog to lick, not wash the sink full of dishes. A dog may ride along on errands, but can't be expected to fetch corn flakes from a shelf where 50 other breakfast cereals are displayed.

I know there are dog-men out there (see Kai's story as told in *Mach* #6), but they are rare. The role of slave with available "dog mode" on command is both more common and easier to live with.

Nonetheless, the important answer here is that you must negotiate first, commit later. If negotiating in detail unhinges the dynamic of play, then play at man and dog in increasing steps—a few hours now, a day later, a weekend at another time—until all the details have been revealed in the action. Then commit, or chase a car down the block and disappear around the corner.

The guy I'm seeing and beating and fucking lately seems to be dropping hints about getting his dog in on the act. I'm wrecked by the idea, but also intrigued. What do people really do with animals and can human relationships survive the tension of anything so extreme?

People who *do* with animals at all do pretty much the same things they do with people. Sucking and being fucked are the usual fare for men who play with dogs or horses. Some dogs learn to lick armpits, dicks, asses, or whole bodies, and others learn to wrestle pretty erotically, but usually an animal is a passive partner in erotic play with any but its own species.

Remember that sex with animals is dangerous, both because of diseases and the unpredictable behavior of animals. Remember that sex with animals is illegal, or at least apt to be perceived as actionable cruelty to the animal. Remember that animals can be injured fairly easily when they are subjected to some kinds of erotic handling. And, above all, remember that animals may be trained to perform sexually, but they can never be said to desire or truly consent to that action.

As for myself, I have a few animal fantasies, but I have chosen in the last couple of decades to animalize appropriately shaggy men and act on my fantasies that way.

All I can say about human relationships surviving anything is this: There is nothing in the world that guarantees the end of a relationship—nothing. Bonnie and Clyde went on loving each other while robbing banks and being shot at by everyone who recognized them. The only cautionary note here has to be that it would probably be hard for a relationship to survive a disagreement over something as extreme as sex with animals *once the act had been performed.* The same can be said for vanilla couples who taste SM, for leather lovers who take a fling with Master-slave dynamics, for any couple that tries anything they consider extreme. If one partner tastes and likes and the other tastes and hates a type of experience, the way back to "the way it was before" can be almost impossible to find.

Do you think it is possible for me to be a good bottom to the man I live with (and love), and a good Top to guys I see from time to time? My lover says I must be a shitty Top, and he feels sorry for the guys I Top, but I feel okay about it all just the way it is.

Surely the way to know if you're a good Top is to check in with your bottoms and yourself. If the bottoms want to see you again, and you feel comfortable with the styles, techniques, and results of your scenes, all is well. You can't afford to be too upset if someone who has never seen you Top has a low opinion of the way you "must" do it.

Even so, if your lover-Top wants to use the fact that you're being a Top elsewhere as a pretext for "putting you in your place" as his bottom at home, why not let him do it? It could be as good for your effort to get into the role as it is for his effort to maintain his role. Of course, you have to be pretty sure of yourself and your skills to bear this "humiliation" and give your lover this liberty. On the other hand, maybe he recognizes that, and maybe he is testing your self-confidence as a way of being sure that you *are* a good (meaning, safe) Top. If you're not, the news of your ineptitude will eventually get out, casting a shadow of doubt over the household your lover is responsible for.

It could also be true that your lover guesses aloud that you are a "shitty" Top in order to help himself get over some perception that your Topping threatens him. It would be nice if everyone were so self-confident and secure that little balancing acts like this were unnecessary. That is not the situation where I live, however, and sometimes the best help we can give someone is to accommodate the effects of his weaknesses and insecurities while we treasure and encourage the exercise of his strengths.

There is nothing about bottoming well that would mean you could not also Top well. On the contrary, the better you are at leathersex, especially the inner dimensions of it, the better you are in all possible roles and techniques once you learn them. Besides, a lot of people alternate between Top and bottom roles all their lives, developing enviable technical skills and confidence on both sides of the paddle, with all success in any form boosting future success in every form.

What's more, some people do *mutual* scenes in which both partners provide and receive stimulation either one after the other or tit-for-tat-as-we-go-along. You might check (diplomatically, of course) whether your lover-Top is trying to goad you into Topping him or getting him into a wrestle-for-Top scene or a mutual scene of some kind.

Warning: Never go out of your way to discover the answer to a question about your partner until you're sure you are able to be equally happy with all possible answers.

8

SAFETY AND HEALTH

Questions about safe play and emergency treatment of injuries don't often come my way. I like to believe that it is because so many of the questions that might be asked are answered in first aid books and classes, even in the front pages of the phone book in most areas. I suppose I know better. People just don't ask these important questions. But, listen to me: Ask! Ask doctors, ask experienced players, ask each other, and read books and take classes. "Play safe" is not just a salutation.

I like being hit with paddles and canes and batons on most of my body, but I've had a few injuries from it. Is there a science to this—places I can say "don't hit here" about while still negotiating a workable scene?

There are definitely places you would be wise to designate as off-limits to any Top who is striking you with any instrument, but the best way to approach the "science" of SM hitting would be to demand that your Tops know what they are doing. In general, you want to have the strokes land on muscle, and to have them avoid bones, tendons, and joints. There is a lot more to it, though. To understand what instruments can be used with how much force on which body parts does not require the mental resources of Albert Einstein. It does, however, require a wide range of information and a certain synthesis of that information that functions almost like instinct.

Where does a Top get such impressive (and thoroughly processed) data? Well, I'd say the *right* source for this is experience—every Top having a history (or alternate current play mode) as a bottom. I have known a few Tops who never apprenticed as bottoms, but—without exception—these guys had tremendous emotional resources and intelligence as well as excellent bottoms from whom they learned as they played. They usually also arrived in the playroom with some special training that included medicine or anatomy.

If, for whatever reason, you can't arrange to take what I am calling the *right* path to safety here, and if you don't have access to classes on the subject or experienced people willing to set aside a few hours to train you and your partner, then you have to learn/ have your partner(s) learn by combining the two hardest and least effective methods: books and experimentation.

Even a few years ago, SM how-to books simply did not exist except in the form of a few privately circulated manuscripts. Now there are several books that contain at least some intentionally instructive material. Books are far from perfect teachers of SM, though, and the authors of SM books don't have board certification or postgraduate degrees in their subjects. Nonetheless, failing all else, collect some books like Jay Wiseman's *SM 101*, my own *Leathersex: A Guide for the Curious Outsider and the Serious Player*, and *The Lesbian S/M Safety Manual* edited by Pat Califia. Read them. Have opinions about what they say. That is, accept nothing as true of yourself if you believe that it is not true, no matter what authority the author cites.

Now, start experimenting. Do not turn this into investigation by trial and error. Instead, settle for investigating through trials that are each only a short step from the previous one, so that it is trial and improved confidence with no need for the discouraging errors. As you go along, report pleasures and unacceptable pains honestly, cautiously invent your own variations, push yourself only enough to keep the experiments hot without making them either confusing or dangerous.

Do not be distracted into the misconception that you must learn to do every SM activity in every book. Do only what you want to do. Do not be misled by the biases of book writers (or friends, or anyone). Judge your results instead by the degree of pleasure you achieve within what you personally consider an acceptable range of risk.

My Top (that's what I call him, not lover) recently suspended me by my wrists and ankles. He tied them all very carefully, gathered the ropes together, and used a chain hoist to lift me off the floor. After a few minutes, the pain in my wrists and shoulders was unbearable. We stopped, and he said we'd try again later. After a week or 10 days, the pains had stopped coming back. Now, a month or so later, he wants to do it again, and wonders what I've done to "toughen myself up" for it. What should I have done?

There is nothing at all that you can do to "toughen up" for this kind of suspension bondage. While I have met a couple of men who could bear being hanged by their hands and feet for short periods, and while I know of ways to give the impression that a man is hanging this way, it is probably best to consider this kind of bondage impossible.

The weakest points in human skeletal anatomy are the joints. That probably seems obvious, but it sometimes goes unnoticed. Putting the kind of weight-driven, directional stress you are talking about on just the wrists and ankles virtually guarantees that one or more of the joints will be damaged in some way. Severe damage is, in fact, probably more likely than the easily healed damage you seem to have suffered.

If a man is given the opportunity to reach past his wrist restraints to hold a certain amount of his weight by grasping the rope or chain above his body, that adds a slight measure of safety. If the restraints are so snug that they also bear a certain amount of the weight by the friction-grip they have on the skin of the forearm or lower leg, that will help a bit as well. If the suspending ropes or chains are spread out in a way that forces the bottom to use his back muscles to some extent to remain suspended (rather than touching the floor or table with his mid back), this will shift the stress on the ankle to a horizontal rather than vertical base pulling against the rope or chain, and things are still a touch safer. And still, all the precautions you can take are inadequate to make this kind of suspension safe.

Very skinny guys who are still strong may be able to bear some seconds of lifting their light body weight on the strength of their wrists and ankles. Even a normal ratio of body weight to strength will make it impossible to hang this way for long, and there are no assurances that any particular body will withstand the practice once, much less repeatedly. So, the best policy here is to find other ways to enjoy suspension.

My favorite suspension system involves ropes or restraints at the ankles, just above the knees, crotch-high on the thighs, around the waist, armpit high on the torso, around the neck (very carefully, of course), and sling-style under the head. Once all these ropes or restraints are in place, I lace them together in three groups—one for legs, one for torso, one for neck and head—and run the three joining ropes through pulls or eye bolts above the body. It takes some practice to learn how to do this, but anyone can work it out in a matter of hours, and then be able to do safe suspension in which the bottom may be laid out level or in any of several safely supported positions.

You might suggest that your Top play around with an idea like this, or, if necessary, tell him I suggested it and ordered you to deliver the suggestion to him.

When I do rope bondage, I keep a pocket knife and bandage scissors at hand in case of emergency. After more than 10 years of wonderfully eventful but safe scenes, I had the emergency. It took several minutes to cut the ropes off. The pocket knife was sharp, but it just pulled the ropes tighter and took forever to saw through them. The scissors just weren't heavy enough for the ropes. What should I have had at hand? This is an urgently important issue, my confidence as a Top is at stake as much as anything.

The importance of this question can hardly be overstated. Like CPR and the Heimlich Maneuver, rapid bondage removal is something everyone who plays ought to know, but might never actually use. The nature of your problem also points up the significance of the word "know." Do not assume you are prepared for emergencies without testing your skills and tools.

You don't have to have an emergency to test yourself. You can check your rope cutting tools every time you get either new ropes or new cutting instruments. If you're using chains and locks, store all locks in a closed position. This forces you to find and use the keys for each lock before using it in a bondage scene. And, with chains and locks, you need two keys per lock and a bolt cutter that has been proven adequate to cut all the chains you use.

What I recommend for quick removal of rope bondage is a three-stage plan. First, learn to do rope bondage that does not have tangles of knots everywhere. The fewer knots, the fewer cuts it will take to actually free the bottom. Second, have a proven pair of scissors at hand. There are some extremely strong paramedic's scissors that can slice through denim seams and leather belts, but they are not the ones usually found in leather stores where the shopkeepers often assume that you and I will balk at the reasonable cost of the best scissors. (Don, a nurse, tells me that you can find these scissors in nursing uniform stores and in the bookstores of colleges and universities where there are medical/nursing or EMT/paramedic programs.) And, finally, have a backup method for rope cutting also at hand. After all, your number-one cutting device may break, fall behind the bed, or just be too greasy to use when you pick it up.

I choose to keep heavy duty bandage scissors and a police emergency knife at hand. The scissors are not the very largest or strongest, but they are comfortably able to cut the ropes I use. The knife has a hook shaped blade which, I am told, was designed to allow rescue workers to reach into a car, easily hook the blade around a seat belt, and pull to cut through the tough nylon web. To use the same knife for our purposes, we hook onto a rope, lift a bit, then get a grip on the rope, folding it tightly around the blade. Holding the rope in this way with the butt of your hand against the bottom's body can be painful for your hand as you pull with the knife, but it prevents you from tightening the ropes on the bottom as you cut them. Don adds that a curved carpet knife, available at any hardware store, will also do the job and, rightly, reminds me to urge you to blunt the sharp thin tip of a carpet knife before putting it in your bondage pack. I would add to Don's comment that only the best and strongest carpet knife should be trusted. I've seen the blades pull out of carpet knives in regular use, but own one that I know would never pull apart.

An important factor of emergency response in a bondage scene is to know when to stall or stop your rescue. The more perfectly the power exchange is working for you and your partner, the more easily you will see whether full removal of the ropes is called for, or just a slight lessening of pressure by, say, cutting the rope around the chest. Over-rescuing destroys the bottom's trust in the Top, just as under-rescuing may leave the bottom in panic even if he is completely safe from damage.

For intense rope bondage scenes in which the bondage itself is the focus of the action, it is even appropriate to mention the style of rescue you want (bottom) or are likely to provide (Top) while setting up the scene. A first-level rescue often involves no rope cutting. Adjusting the position of a rope, just assuring the bottom that he is still being watched, or a hug that presses the ropes against the bottom's body may be all that a mild panic requires. Of course, if the bottom has been injured or has passed out, the bondage should come off instantly, and you will be able to achieve that easily with your pre-tested tools at hand.

Can I just grit my teeth and scream through it if I get an attack of claustrophobia during a bondage or encasement scene? So far, I haven't let anyone do much bondage on me, but my fantasies include being tied or wrapped and put in a box or coffin. So my question is, how do I deal with claustrophobia, other than avoiding tight spaces?

It might seem surprising, even to yourself, to hear yourself fantasizing about encasements and coffins while worrying about a potentially uncontrollable fear of tight spaces. Odd as it sounds, the combination seems to be fairly common.

This is certainly a question for a mental health professional, which I am not, but I am happy to share what I have gathered from experience. One, screaming through a fear doesn't seem to work. It just exhausts your physical and emotional resources, making you less able to cope with the waves of irrational fear. Two, reasoning your way through the fear only seems to be any help at all if you are able to do your reasoning out loud with the person who will be in charge of your encasement, and therefore have the option of removing it if necessary. Three, the best approach seems to be a combination of reasoning it out with your partner (but not psycho-babbling to the point that either of you are lying to keep up) and doing the scene you want by degrees.

Here's an example of what I mean: After hearing about your conflicting fears and fantasies, I might have you examine the materials with which I intend to encase (mummify) you. We'd talk about how I can still see your movements, hear the sounds you make, etc. after the mummification is done. We'd then wrap just parts of your body. The legs and feet below the knees are usually a good first step, while wrapping the arms to the torso and hips is often too extreme a beginning. And, bit by bit, in one evening or several, we'd work you through it until you were able to get all wrapped up. Maybe the bits that scared you most would even be "faked" at first. If you had a problem about your head being wrapped, we might just drop a T-shirt over your face and tuck it under your head. If you were able to get used to that, we might tie the shirt to make a loose bag to be pulled over your head. Next, we might add a few strips of tape over the shirt, and so on. By always being ready to back up a few degrees, and with appropriate encouragement, I bet you'd be reveling in your claustrophobia in no time.

I've been warned—in magazines and local classes/demos—not to leave a bottom in bondage unattended, but I do it all the time, for hours at a time. Why shouldn't I?

This is one of the aspects of safe, sane, consensual play that seems to distress a lot of guys, and that includes some new players and young men as well as the older, more seasoned Tops. Having had a few disquieting experiences over the years, I have become a subscriber to the idea that a bottom in bondage should always be in the attention of someone able to remove the bondage rapidly. The idea is purely a matter of being prepared for all the unpredictable "what-ifs" in the world. What if the bottom panics? What if the bottom has a heart attack? What if the house catches fire? What if there's an earthquake? What if your bondage suddenly changes in a way you didn't intend because the bottom moves, a rope stretches or breaks, etc.? What if absolutely any unlikely thing goes wrong in any way *and you, the Top, are not there to deal with it*?

Think the possibilities through very, very carefully. Consider honestly what you know and believe about your skills, your materials, your bottom, and everything, including what kind of luck the gods are showering on you. Then determine to what extent you are willing to put yourself and your bottom at risk. As I said above, my choice has finally settled on the rule of no unsupervised bondage, but I am willing to make exceptions for short periods of time under rare circumstances.

I've always had a few beers or a couple of bourbon drinks before I play, and I've been playing for nearly 20 years. Nowadays, guys don't want to go into the playroom if I stop at the bar on the way. If we meet in a bar, they want to make a date for a later, nondrinking time. Do you drink? Do you think a couple of beers make an experienced Top dangerous?

Yes, I drink. No, I don't think "a couple of beers make an experienced Top dangerous." And now I'm wondering why you are having this experience. My own experience suggests that most bottoms are relatively realistic about Tops, judging their mental acuity and emotional clarity by observation rather than tossing them out purely because they are known to have had a drink or two.

Is it possible that your judgement and behavior are being altered more than you think by your "couple" of bourbons? Is it possible that you have a history of overdrinking which is known in your community? Even one scene made dangerous by drinking is enough to destroy a player's reputation, and rightly so, I think.

It seems to me that you should check with the bartenders, if you know them, at your local bar. Ask them what is said about you, assuring them that you are not going to punch them out for telling you the truth. If anyone knows your reputation as a drinker, the bartenders do.

If I am misreading the situation, understand that I have no intention to offend, but I can't help being surprised that your experience differs so greatly from my own. What's more, it is my opinion that it is always better for all concerned if the question of drinking is settled by choosing sobriety every time the question comes up at all.

I am not one of those people who want to live as long as possible at any cost, but I am HIV- and healthy, and I want to stay this way. What kind of safe sex guidelines do you suggest for a hungry, piggy bottom who also wants to continue being a hungry, piggy bottom?

Safe sex is safe sex. It is no different for a hungry, piggy bottom than for a quiet-living, middle-aged accountant. In fact, the accountant and the pig could easily enough be the same guy in different guises, no?

Most leathersex tends to be less about fucking than about sensations and sensual experience provided by toys and mind games, so we start out in the playroom with a lot of options that carry no significant risk of transmitting any disease organism. Also, since leathermen have to learn to control and monitor risks of physical and psychological damage, they are more likely to be willing to be realistic also about risks involving micro-organisms. (That's my theory, anyway.)

Stay up to date as to what the most informed authorities consider safe, remain realistic about what risks you are willing to take, and make your choices. Find ways to disinfect your toys, and otherwise manage the risk of transmitting disease organisms on equipment (See the question below and others in this book and in *Leather and Latex Care* by Kelly J. Thibault.). Then, having established your personal guidelines, do not be encouraged, by drugs, alcohol, seductive players, or the pace of a scene, to break your own rules.

Is it really necessary for whips, canes, and even dildos to be one-bottom toys?

Frankly your hierarchy of toys here seems a bit skewed. I'd say that dildos are more likely to call for a one-bottom rule than whips and canes.

It is purely a matter of whether the toys can be adequately cleaned and disinfected between uses and users. If they can, there is no need to restrict their use by other bottoms. If not, a single-user designation is the safest choice. This brings us to the question of what is adequately clean and how toys are to be disinfected between users.

Building my own plans around the best information I have been able to get, what I do with dildos is this: I only use insertable toys that can be either discarded after use or washed in the hot cycle of my dishwasher. I have friends who assert that all I am doing is infecting my dishwasher, but I believe my actions are adequate since I set aside every dishwasher-cleaned toy for at least a few days of air drying before it is reused. When I am playing with a new bottom, I use condoms on my toys until I know that he also accepts my conviction that the dishwasher cycle plus days of air drying equals completely safe toys.

I have lots of toys that have been improvised specifically to accommodate my own sense of what is safe. I used to keep bundles of thin bamboo skewers with permanently built-in handles. They're great for pounding and scratching and sensitizing, but they usually draw blood. In recent years, I buy cheap skewers at less than a buck for a hundred, tie them together with rubber bands or bits of scrap leather, and discard them after one use as scratching or scraping toys. I have also chosen not to replace some kinds of ass toys exclusively because they could not be run through the hot cycle in a dishwasher. And, I have made arrangements with friends who own autoclaves to disinfect some of my toys (like sounds and steel catheters) between uses. In fact, I feel sure that the dishwasher and air drying is adequate for sounds, and I do that when I am playing with guys who agree that it is adequate for *their* sense of safety.

I never argue the safety question with anyone. If a guy feels that his urethra should only be penetrated by a sound that has been autoclaved, I pull out a sound that is still in its autoclaved wrapper.

Toys, like some canes and many paddles, that have appropriately nonporous surfaces, can be washed and disinfected easily. The soaps and disinfectants used in hospitals have distinctly antisexy scents, but can be used between scenes and away from the playroom, or—as I see it—adequately replaced by less obnoxious household products.

Nurse Don adds this note: Latex, rubber, metal, and most other nonporous surfaces can be easily and thoroughly disinfected with a simple solution of 10 percent household bleach. Mix 1/4 cup household liquid bleach with 2¼ cups tap water. Then soak your toys for 5 to 6 seconds, or apply with a sponge. Let the toys sit for 2 to 3 minutes. Rinse well with clear water and dry. Wear gloves to protect your hands. Do not use bleach on cloth or leather, or on any other porous materials.

Certain of the hepatitis viruses are *very* hardy, and can survive for days or even weeks on dry porous surfaces unless they have been chemically disinfected or exposed to prolonged high heat (such as a dishwasher).

My answer about how to clean whips and other leather toys appears below.

How do you disinfect a bloody whip so it can be used again without carrying HIV from one bottom to another?

Safety And Health

This question has occasioned a good deal of discussion and more than a little disagreement in leathersex communities all around the country. Any answer will seem to err on the side of caution to some players while seeming insufficiently careful to others. So, knowing that I am creating enemies, I will tell you what seems right to me. It does no good to go looking for medically expert opinions: the few I have encountered run the gamut from certainty that a drop of blood on a whip means it ought to be destroyed to an equally certain assurance that there is nothing to worry about because whips cannot carry sufficient body fluids or convey them quickly enough from person to person.

I continue to believe in air drying as the primary means of destroying HIV on toys, but I am well aware that other microbes (as likely to be picked up from the floor, sweaty skin, or my hands as from infected blood) are harder to destroy. So, I wash my whips quickly but thoroughly with hot water and a stiff suds of anti-bacterial hand soap. Then I press the water out of the leather with layers of clean towels, and hang the whip to start drying. When it is dry enough that I don't imagine I'll be trapping water inside the leather, I condition with bag balm or dubbin, wiping away the excess after just a few minutes. Then I like to let the whip dry for at least a day or so, though usually it comes out to weeks (dammit!), before I use it again.

Bag balm is an antiseptic salve intended to be used on the chapped udders of milk cows. It's sort of like petroleum jelly and lanolin with something called 8-hydroxyquinoline sulfate in it. Farmers and veterinarians have found lots of uses for bag balm, and lots of leathermen have as well. Dubbin is a lanolin-based product originally made to condition hard saddle leathers. It is sometimes sold in modern leather(sex) shops with a black pigment suspended in it, which is convenient now that just about everyone's leathers are black.

For *all the details* you could ever want about the cleaning of leather (like whips and floggers), again, I recommend you pick up

Kelly Thibault's *Leather and Latex Care* (Daedalus Publishing Company, 1996).

Is watersports inherently unsafe? You can't stop me from drinking piss by saying "yes," but I want to know the truth. If staying alive and free of disease means not getting pissed IN, who needs it. Cum is sacramental, piss is holy water, abs are altars, and if I must, I will be the sacrifice . . . but I'd just as soon not.

It is my conviction that piss is not inherently unsafe. Granted, the study on which I originally based the public statement of this opinion is growing old, but I have heard of no specific study that contradicts it. So, I refer you to *The Journal of Infectious Diseases*, December 1989, in which a study conducted jointly by Tufts University and the Harvard School of Medicine is reported. Their conclusion was that no "replication quality" HIV organisms survived in urine.

You should remember, however, that the bugs involved in infections of the bladder and urethra can survive in piss since they originate in a urine-wet environment and/or are introduced to the piss stream immediately before it leaves the body. I have always taken some comfort in the fact that infections of the bladder and urethra are discomforting at best, and usually painful during urination, meaning they would hardly go unnoticed. Nor do I think the discomforts of such infections would lead a man to consider pissing sexy.

As with any safety information or safe sex guidelines, you will inevitably be responsible for your own choices and actions, so I strongly recommend that you not make your decisions based solely on the ones I have made for myself.

Is blood-sucking leathersex, and can it be done safely in the age of AIDS? I'm not a blood sucker myself, but my most exciting

scenes have been with a couple of guys who do it, and I am HIV+. (They know my status, and still want my blood oozing around and in their mouths.)

As to whether *anything* is or is not properly defined as leathersex, I leave that entirely up to the players involved. If they say they are participating in leathersex, they are, and the question needs no further investigation. If you and I would say that what they do looks like or fails to look like leathersex, we are at best guessing, at worst imposing our opinions on others to no good purpose.

I'd guess, though, that most folks who involve blood in their sexual activities in any way would at least accept some non-mainstream definition of themselves or their actions. Maybe kinky is a more apt term, or perhaps the people engaged in blood sucking think of themselves as fetishists. As long as both or all participants either agree or remain silent on the subject of labeling the activity, the words don't matter much.

HIV does matter, however, and it seems to me that the question of whether blood sucking is AIDS-safe or not is an extreme case version of the question of whether cocksucking with orgasm is safe. Since this is an area of tremendous controversy in 1995, there is a great deal of information being published on the subject. Read the pro and con comments of AIDS experts on cocksucking and cum eating with an understanding of the fact that we believe there is always HIV present in the blood of infected individuals, but we know that the ejaculate of infected individuals will not always carry sufficient HIV to transmit infection. This means, as I see it, that *if getting cum in your mouth is dangerous*, blood sucking is similarly dangerous, only much more so. If cum eating is low risk or no risk, there remains the possibility that blood sucking is unsafe. To determine that blood in the mouth is definitely presenting no risk of HIV transmission would involve the kind of study that you and I know will not be undertaken by modern medical scientists. Or, allowing my cynicism to show, it would require studies you and I would never hear of if they were undertaken, particularly if the finding was that the practice was safe.

Is it okay to lick the bottoms of boots, the soles? For that matter, can shoe polish and the other greases and things used on boots be bad for me?

As far as I am able to determine, the licking of boots, including the soles and the recently polished leather parts, presents no risks but the mechanical ones. You might, for example, cut your tongue or lip on the sharp edge of a new boot sole, or pull a few whiskers by catching them in an eyelet. On the other hand, licking or being exposed to some of the things that might accumulate on boots is another matter altogether.

Think of all the things that might collect in tiny but potentially significant amounts on the soles and lower edges of a boot on a typical sidewalk. You have to start with the piss and shit of dogs, maybe people, but the list goes on to include any number of rotten things like food spit out because it's rotten. Then there's spit, sputum, snot, the drool of garbage bags, and the drippings of automobile fluids. Beyond these things, the list could actually get ugly.

As a Top who enjoys boot service, but a man who does not want to contribute unthinkingly to anyone else's trouble, I have developed habits that include refusing to let a boy lick my boots unless I am pretty convinced they are more or less clean. And, when I suspect I am with a boy who is HIV+ I can become very pushy about this. My slave warren was required to greet me by kissing my boots every time he saw me, but he was trained to keep those kisses on the tops of my boots. We both enjoyed more extensive boot licking scenes, too. So, sometimes I had him scrub my boots. Later, before I'd been outside, we'd get boot-crazed, leaving his face smeared with polish and my boots dripping with his spit, including the soles. Other times, for variety, I'd wash my boots myself and surprise him with an intense boot scene, with the surprise adding a nice edge to the play.

Frankly, I suppose I am obsessing over a fairly slight risk, but I became very particular about clean boots or severely limited licking when I discovered the special dangers posed for HIV+ people by bird and cat shit. Tops, of course, can manage all of this without letting bottoms in on their cleaning efforts. Bottoms can handle it by developing a scene style that includes the non-tongue cleaning of the boots up front. Or, I guess, people can decide to take their chances.

Can I get athlete's foot in my mouth from sucking toes?

Supposing that the fungus you're calling athlete's foot can infect your mouth, I don't think it would still be called athlete's foot—maybe foot-and-mouth disease instead. But, knowing nothing that would help me answer this question, I presented it to a doctor. He was baffled at first, but ended up saying that he was "fairly certain that at least some of the fungus infections that occur on feet and between toes" could presumably survive and become sustained infections "in the corners of the mouth, perhaps in the nostrils." He expressed a greater concern that HIV+ individuals might complicate the already complex oral fungus problems that are frequently associated with HIV infection.

An *experienced* friend of mine is more definite: "I'm convinced it happens."

I know, this doesn't really amount to an answer. What it does amount to is also valuable, though. It is a warning, a suggestion that foot sucking should probably be avoided if the feet you are offered show any sign of infection.

If I've been vaccinated for hepatitis, does that make rimming safe? Scat, too?

Very simply, no. Rimming and scat without impenetrable barriers are not disease-safe activities, and there is nothing you can do to make them disease safe. I am not saying don't do what you want to, only that you should not pretend to yourself that what you are doing is safe.

Meantime, if you're going to be licking assholes or making contact with shit, do anything and everything that you can to reduce the risks. Starting out as germ free as you are able to be is a step in the right direction. Playing with partners who are as healthy as possible is a giant step in the same laudable direction. Cleaning up thoroughly as soon after the scene as possible is another important risk-reduction tactic. Of course, you'll want to be as vaccinated and healthy as possible yourself, and you'll want to play in physical surroundings that are not going to trap and retain micro-bugs, allowing them to continue their attacks for days or weeks after the scene.

I know at least one person who feels about scat the way the piss-safety questioner above does about watersports: He'd rather not live if he can't be smeared with the shit of a hot man at least once in a while. This attitude colors his decisions about what he finds acceptable risk, but it does not change the actual risk level.

I've been told repeatedly that electricity above the waist is dangerous, but I've seen guys using violet wands on other guys' chests. Now, I hear there are commercially available, electric tit clamps. If they're safe, I want them. Are they safe?

The violet wand, which I understand is best described as "radio-frequency static" (whatever that means), is equally safe on all parts of the body, with the *possible exception of the eyeball.* It arcs superficially and, as such, cannot interfere with biologically essential electrical impulses. Be warned that you can burn the skin and, with a certain amount of concentration, also damage deeper tissues with the violet wand. This requires concentration, but it can happen, whether it is intended or not.

As for electrical tit clamps, they do exist, and there is no reason to think they are unsafe. Don't go trying to electrify your favorite tit clamps, though. What makes the commercially available clamps so assuredly safe is that they are insulated, bipolar clamps. The two "lips" of each clamp are the positive and negative poles of a single circuit, so the power is not running free inside the chest, it's just darting across the space pinched by the clamp, usually just a nipple.

Actually, although I am not going to try to explain it all here, electricity above the waist probably involves fewer dangers than you've heard, and more pleasures than you've imagined. I am not saying there are no possible problems, only that what is safe is a much broader range of options than anyone is able to write out or teach in an evening. If you really want to learn about electricity, it's one of the few techniques that really requires a hand-to-hand transmission of the most desirable information.

How do you determine when an emergency in the playroom is a setback that just needs a bit of time and when it needs a trip to the ER?

This is not a question that can be answered in any universal way, but it can't be ignored either. I believe that everyone should have some first-aid training, and any training you could get would help you to recognize conditions that require more attention than you are prepared or able to give. Another form of essential preparation for serious play is to be as informed as you are able about your partner's medical needs, physical differences, etc. Again, the information can be very useful in identifying conditions that are, so to say, normal for that person, and recognizing situations where professional help is called for.

With or without training and proper preparation, an emergency may arise. The most likely emergency I am aware of is fainting. When a person faints, you want to get them lying out flat and unencumbered *immediately*. Prop the feet up, cool the head or splash the face with water. If the person is not coming around within a minute, call for help. Understand that it is better to turn the paramedics away at the door, perhaps embarrassed, than to call them too late when something serious has happened.

The next most likely emergency I can think of is severe bleeding. If the bleeding is characterized by spurting, an artery is probably cut. In the case of arterial bleeding or if the bleeding doesn't stop right away with local pressure, get the person to an emergency room. Please, don't resort to a tourniquet unless you know from special training what you are doing. A badly applied tourniquet can be the cause of a lot of damage.

It would be possible to give you a dab of information about this, that, and the other thing, but what is really more useful is to send you off to find the training you ought to have. If, for whatever reason, you are unwilling to get extensive first-aid training, at least get a good book on first aid and read it, over and over till you know what it says.

Playroom safety is everyone's responsibility. Tops may be in a position to need and use the information more often than bottoms, but not by much. Bottoms may need to deal with their own medical emergencies, with those of Tops, or with those of others in a group or party situation. What we do can be done with an amazing degree of safety, considering what it is that we do, but no one has the right to be unprepared for emergencies.

9

PSYCHE, SPIRIT, AND THE SOCIAL CREATURE

The range of questions in this chapter is remarkable, but the questions belong together, if only loosely, nonetheless. Here men question their responsibility to themselves, God, church, each other, their political and social values, and to the higher selves they know only in rare moments. If these questions go unanswered—and the questions like them in each of our lives—we are not well and cannot claim to be capable of safe and sane leathersex.

I usually can't be bothered with what a few of my friends call "aftercare check-ins" and visits. Do you think this makes me a less good Top?

I think that a good Top has three periods of responsibility: preparation, performance, and follow-through. The preparation may be seen as nothing more than undertaking only scenes you know you can handle with equipment (if any) you have learned to use. At other times, obviously, preparation can be something quite complex, as with public kidnapings or intense medical scenes. Performance includes being responsible for all the elements of the scene as it progresses, primarily the pleasure both parties hope to achieve safely. (My own version of this is that I take full responsibility for my own pleasure, which ought to result in the experience the bottom is seeking as well, if I am with the right bottom.) Follow-through, or aftercare, is no less important.

The importance of aftercare depends very much on how you play, how intensely you play, and with whom you play. Tops unaccustomed to the idea of aftercare often get the impression that its purpose is to be sure that no injuries or infections have developed as a result of the scene. This concept of after-scene attention is completely mistaken. Of course, a Top must take a caring interest in such possibilities, and should be as prepared as he is able to deal with them, and at the very least he has to put himself in a position to know of any injuries or infections he has permitted or caused. This may be interesting and important information, but it is often something the Top is going to be unable to do much about unless he is a qualified doctor or nurse. What a Top should be checking in about is confusion, lingering psychological effects of the bottom's scene experience, the possible development of mental or emotional "infections" such as misplaced anger or questions of self-worth. And, no less important, the Top should be checking that he has not done something during the scene that may have been safe but which the bottom considers "wrong."

Granted, most Tops are not going to accept that they are wrong in terms of techniques used during scenes just because a bottom reports that they are. Nonetheless, it is very useful to know, for future reference, that such and such activity strikes a bottom as wrong when he has had time to consider and reflect on the scene.

Just as some people misconstrue the basic purpose of after-scene attentions, others misconstrue the role of the Top in such conversations. A Top is not necessarily a psychiatrist, psychologist, or even a capable peer counselor, and should not yield to the temptation to offer help he is not qualified to give. So, why bother checking in at all? Without overstepping the limitations of friendship or claiming any nonexistent skills, a Top can often answer questions for a bottom, clear up confusion, or—just by checking in—put the lie to the appearance of uncaring brutality in the scene. Only experience will teach you when aftercare is and is not useful, but it never hurts to be available in case there are questions. Besides, for the sake of Rule One, you want to be sure that you have left the bottom still ready to play again, if not with you then with someone else.

In fact, making an "official" check-in call often pushes a troubled bottom to sublimate or hide his problems with the scene, the style of play, or with the Top. It is usually sufficient, and often better, to call or drop by and say something like, "I really got high from the scene Friday night and I'm looking forward to a repeat performance." The bottom's response to such a simple statement may assure you that all is well, particularly if he says, "I am too, Sir." Or, it may tip you off that something is amiss, especially if the bottom has the wherewithal to say so plainly.

Aftercare is less likely to be needed for people who play together often, and "official" check-ins are probably replaced by frequent social interactions for people who see each other in social situations as often as they see each other in the dungeon. When a scene has gone very well, and there has been some straight time afterwards—like a night of cuddling and a breakfast—the fact that aftercare is not needed may be obvious.

Aftercare is, for reasons that seem none too mysterious, more likely to be needed when a scene has involved a level of play that is unusual for either party. And, although exactly the opposite might seem to be the case, an "official" check-in may be needed when a live-in couple does something that is unusual or particularly intense. The special reason for live-ins to set aside intentionally devised aftercare time is that scenes tend to escalate in any given direction, especially if the Top enjoys that direction. The only real safeguard against having this escalation run to extremes that are not really desired is to insure that the bottom's reactions are carefully and fully reported on a regular basis.

By now you know whether I would think you a less good Top if you ignore or avoid aftercare. When it is called for, it is an important part of the Top's role in the scene and in the community of leathersex players. When it is not needed, it can safely be skipped, but I wonder if there is ever a time when it is completely safe to be unavailable to the bottom who, at a later time, might discover a need to discuss what he has experienced.

Are leather faeries real leathermen?

Who is and who is not a real leatherman has to have something to do with what each of those words means to you, and what they mean when used together. It is my inclination to leave each person free to define himself, if he wants to do so, then to use his (or her) self-identification as a known-truth. If a dyke wants to be him/he/a man, so be it. If a spanking bottom wants not to be thought an SM player, so be it.

More specifically, but not very significantly, I have seen a lot of self-identified faeries doing scenes that would frighten the usual leather bar patron. What I suggest is that you determine for yourself whether you are a real leatherman, and accord to everyone else the same freedom to identify himself.

How do I as a bottom relate to Tops when I see them socially, even entirely away from leather context?

Courtesy is never a mistake. Courtesy, pressed in the direction it already leads, to the greatest extreme good taste permits, can include enough respectful deference to put the ball in his court. What's more, followed with some caution, this plan can be carried out so that no one else is aware of any special communication between you and Mr. Top. Not every leatherman is prepared to acknowledge his leather life in all social situations, even if he is a famous Master, but no one is going to be offended by good manners and decent marks of respect.

Imagine yourself in this situation: In 1976, a bottom we will call X was the guest of honor at a university dinner. Halfway through dinner, he noticed Y, a Top he had recently been beaten by. Y was serving the table next to X's, and would shortly be delivering desserts to X's own table. Poor bottom X was at a loss for a course of action. He considered going to the men's room, but had already used that excuse to leave the table 10 minutes earlier to call and confirm a date for later that night. What he chose to do might give you some material for inventing instant strategies in the future.

Fortunately, the Top and bottom had recently had serious discussions of the subjects the bottom was then lecturing about at the university. So, when the waiter-Top arrived at the table, the bottom turned to his host, a huffing, grey professor, and said, "I am very surprised to have the opportunity to introduce you to a very good friend. . . ." When the waiter looked a tad flustered, trying to offer a handshake while balancing a tray, the bottom-guest of honor, popped up saying, "Allow me," and took the tray. As the bottom passed around the table, allowing professors and wives to take their own desserts, no one saw anything amiss. Finally, at his own place, the bottom let the host's wife serve the last two places. The Top was still chatting with each couple as he was introduced to them, sounding quite expert in the subject of the evening. He was obviously clear that a little stalling would be useful.

In the end, the bottom managed to pass the empty tray to another passing waiter. The Top-waiter caught up with and retrieved his tray a few yards short of the kitchen, and was in another part of the room during coffee service.

Generally the situation is less acute. Tops and bottoms,

however, must be accorded exactly equal freedom to avoid unwanted revelations and embarrassing publicity about their private lives. Often, simple courtesy suffices. It is never appropriate to force someone in a nonleather environment to mention or recognize his intimate, leathersex familiarity with you. Granted, this can be difficult if you know someone only as, say, Master Jack. Perhaps his name is not even Jack in the everyday world, but a little care, and a willingness to suffer the very slight discomfort of having "mis-remembered" his name will carry you through that situation. I am not so politically ignorant that I think it is a good general rule for people who know each other only in leathersex contexts to pretend not to know each other at all in public or in nonleather social situations.

As a bottom, since you asked your question that way, it is usually not difficult at all to find ways to demonstrate respect for a Top without spilling secret beans. Nor is it difficult in most situations to telegraph that you are open to a free exchange of familiarities and information, leaving the decision and first step in the Top's hands, not because he is the Top but because this gives both parties equal opportunity to reveal or keep secret the information in question.

When in Rome, it is said, do as the Romans do. Similarly, when in Vanilla-land, do as the Vanillans do unless you are assured by the leather acquaintance you meet that a more relaxed exchange is mutually acceptable. It really isn't a question of who's on top; it is a question of who is less at liberty in the situation.

I'm gay, but I recently let a straight woman flog me at a party. Then she sucked me off, and I got into that. Next time she sees me (at the same party next month, I expect) she says she's going to beat me senseless and make me eat her cunt. I'm excited by this plan. Am I turning straight?

It is my opinion that most gay men are incapable of turning

straight, and recent biological investigations seem to be on the brink of proving me right. On the other hand, I suspect that you have actually misstated your question. Rather than “Am I turning straight?” maybe you would be better off asking, “Can my gay identity survive cross-orientation play?” To this, the answer is a simple yes.

You may eventually discover that you are comfortable with, even eager to embrace a new identity as a bisexual. That is not necessarily what is going to happen, though. Gay men can certainly remain gay men while having sex or scenes or both with women. There may be political complications involved, depending on the community you live in, but who needs to be PC in the dungeon or, for that matter, the bedroom.

A lot of people who know me well think that I should “admit” I'm bisexual, but I'm not. I am a gay man who happens to have fallen in love with women a couple of times. If one of those relationships had lasted the rest of my life, I'd still have considered myself a gay man to my dying day on the basis of my view of myself, which is not too directly tied to the sex or identity of my partners.

Whole books have been written on the subject of sexual identity, and I have heard plenty of lectures and discussions about orientation identity in conflict with sexual behavior. In my view this topic is a classic case of the question and all possible answers being purely academic. After a lot of academic study, someone may publish a theory that someone else may find useful, but people will manage to have good sex in the meantime without any scholarly stamp of approval on their choice of partners.

Keep it simple. Do what turns you on. Identify yourself to yourself in whatever way feels honest and works for you consistently. And leave the conceptual juggling and label writing to someone who has a doctoral thesis committee to please.

I've heard of something called "Top's Disease," and I think I know what it is, but maybe not. And I wonder, are there equivalents: bottom's disease, slave's disease, Master's disease, etc.?

As far as I know, the idea of Top's Disease was born in classes taught by Sybil Holiday and Bill Henkin, and I can't presume to give their original definition as my answer. So, here's my take on the words as I've heard them used in the San Francisco leathersex community: It appears that Top's Disease is generally understood to mean the habit (or occasional behavior) of expecting to be accorded all the time and by everyone the deference you demand of a bottom in a scene. In short, it is a twisted form of arrogance, a failure of manners.

I have certainly found a similar dysfunction in Masters, bottoms, and slaves. When it occurs in Masters it is easily recognized as the same disgusting preoccupation with one's own superiority that is Top's Disease. When it is seen in bottoms and slaves it seems the disease is most often encouraged, for reasons that reveal weaknesses in others. A servile bottom, for example, who scrambles around underfoot seeking to humble himself before everyone is often seen as "dedicated" to his lifestyle or role, spoken of as somehow a "more real" slave because of it. No one seems to remember at the time that erotic slavery is a dynamic in which a responsible Master or Mistress has a vital role. In fact, Top's Disease—understood as expecting his own will to have the same prominence in all situations that it is given in scenes—is no different when it infects bottoms or slaves. They are demanding the recognition and attention from others that they want in scenes.

It is realistically possible among leatherfolk for certain forms of respect and recognition to influence the ways we behave toward each other outside the play space. What makes the difference between dysfunction and courtesy is whether the behavioral indicators are demanded or coerced on the one hand or simply come to be freely given among people sufficiently familiar with each other.

In a fairly close circle of friends, I always expect my slaves to be recognized as slaves. For any friend to do anything that could be considered serving my slave distresses me. It is not that I would allow others to make demands on my slave or presume that he is there to serve anyone but me. But, he and I can both feel good about the dynamics revealed if other Tops request that I permit him to do something or other for them. At a party, for example, one of the standard rules of being my slave is that anyone I am talking with will be served as I am in the sense of having drinks brought, packages carried, errands run for them, so long as this activity does not interfere with my slave's service to me. This keeps the energy of the scene and relationship up and running, and helps others experience our closeness and the nature of our relationship. When other Tops (or anyone, for that matter) make a demand directly on my slave without my permission, the rule is clear. My slave is to report the idiot to me immediately, even if it means telling me about a man's bad behavior right in front of that man.

I may or may not be willing to allow another man to use my electric shaver, but I certainly don't want him using it without my explicit permission. Nor would I ever presume to use an electric shaver that I happened to see at someone's house without being sure whose shaver it was and that the owner meant for me to be allowed to use it. Exactly the same attitude applies to slaves and bottoms, and should be expected of Tops and Masters.

If I write to a hot Topman I've seen in mags and public events, how do I address him without over-bottoming or showing too little respect?

Writing a letter to any stranger is much the same. Presume nothing at all. The "hot Topman" may actually be a bottom or slave, he may be in a relationship which would be distressed by an inappropriate letter, or he may be a 100 percent vanilla model who just happens to work in leather because it looks good on him (and the resulting pictures sell well). I have actually even known a number of guys who are completely heterosexual who've done gay porn photo sessions. So, you see, any assumptions can be bad guesses.

In the case of a gay male leathersex video I worked on a few years ago, the Top looked great in the leathers, but they were borrowed for the shoot. In fact, he had next to no knowledge of leathersex, and was even frightened that the watered-down little smacks and whacks he was asked to give the (genuine) bottom were somehow wrong or dangerous. Pictures from that day were published in several magazines, and I'd be very surprised if he didn't get a good deal of fan mail from bottoms.

When you write to any stranger, identify yourself clearly, state your reason for writing clearly, and give the person you are addressing permission to disregard your letter if it seems importunate or in any way inappropriate. Don't write, "Even if you don't want to hear from me again, answer my letter and tell me so or I will have to write again until I am sure you have read one of my letters." I have personally received such notes many times. My own habit is to ignore the first letter, and return the second one unread. It sometimes gets worse. A guy writes an irritating letter. If there is a second one, I return it, then he gets angry and goes out of his way to try to make something of my arrogance (not giving him my attention) in public. This kind of behavior is disturbing to everyone forced to witness it, and it achieves nothing for anyone.

The reasonable and, I would say, right way to approach a stranger by mail is not the least bit different for Tops or bottoms. In the absence of a personal relationship—no, fantasy relationships don't count, no matter how many times you have shot your wad on a guy's picture!—every unsolicited communication is an intrusion, made excusable only if you arrive with compliments which are the written equivalent of a tasteful bouquet of flowers. Barging in with effusive praise that may be the verbal equivalent of gaudy gifts is not recommended.

What it comes down to is nothing more difficult than this: be nice.

I have a political problem. I'm a Republican, time-tested and party-approved, and I'm a leathersex bottom. I feel like my lives are incompatible, but I can't change either one. What am I to do?

Go on about your business as though your political preferences had nothing to do with your sexual identity. Come to think of it, the two are not related in any direct way. Is a bottom's or Top's performance changed in any way by the fact that he is registered to vote as a Democrat, Republican, Green Party Member, or Libertarian? I think not. Discussing your politics or arguing with other people's politics may make you less popular in many leather circles, but not all. In the company of reasonable leathermen, your politics will be ignored if you are a good and reliable player. A poor bottom might easily think that his politics (or the color of his house or the kind of car he drives or . . .) is the reason he isn't getting beaten and fucked, only to discover that playing better makes the problem go away.

The truth, by the way, is that the gay male leather community used to be something like the politically conservative branch of the gay community, and I wouldn't be too surprised to discover that it still is, relatively speaking. I am not likely to make such a discovery unless I wake up psychic one morning, but I know beyond any doubt that politics are irrelevant to strange bedfellows if they find each other sufficiently attractive.

Is it possible to become addicted to SM? I feel that I am a candidate for this delightful or dangerous addiction.

I am tempted to go to the *DSM*, the manual used by mental health care providers, for a definition of addiction, but I won't. Let me offer my own definition as a way for you to work out your own answer to your question. Addiction—according to Joseph W. Bean who is not a doctor of any sort—is an overpowering urge for anything which, because of its nature or the degree of the urge or the frequency with which it must be satisfied, interferes with the person's ability to function successfully in his life, particularly when the interference reduces his ability to earn a living, care for his body and surroundings properly, or to establish and maintain satisfactory intimate relationships.

Does your involvement with SM fit this definition? If so, I'd say you need to find a mental health professional and ask for help, but be sure to find one who will not assume that your interest in SM is, of itself, a treatable illness. If you don't feel you fit the definition, try to track down the source of the concern that caused you to ask this question. You might still want to seek help, but the nature of the help may be different than you originally suspected.

The fact that your question precedes any immediate concern (since you call yourself a "candidate" rather than an addict) encourages me to believe you are a thinking and introspective person. Thinking is good. Introspection is not always bad. But I'd advise you to put these characteristics to work digesting a few books that will give you a good framework for further thought and self-discovery. Guy Baldwin's *Ties That Bind* and Mark Thompson's anthology *Leatherfolk* would be a superior starting point.

I can understand that sex and spirituality are related, but I can't see *how* in a way that makes sense. Can you help me?

Sex and spirituality, as it seems to me, are powerfully linked in at least two primary ways. First, the sexual impulse is intertwined with human yearnings for continuity and even a form of immortality (offspring), which makes sex a material response to a spirit-perceived need. Second, sex is among the human activities that can provide access to ecstatic states in which the time-locked, material view can sometimes be transcended or (if only rarely) replaced by a deeper and broader view of reality, one that is indistinguishable from the visions of the mystics.

Any number of writers have composed books about this one question. Purusha Larkin's *Divine Androgyne* comes to mind and, although not related to leathersex particularly, the poetry of James Broughton is often directly relevant to the question of how sex and spirit are linked.

No one in modern times or recent centuries has produced anything to compare with the opening chapters of the Bible. There, by engaging a capacity to read the material afresh rather than merely reflecting on the standard scholarship, we see that the ancient thinkers believed that many of the elements we see as defining us as human beings were initiated at the same moment. Sex, death, human will, and the first reasons to strive for higher states of being and a better relationship with God, according to the writers of Genesis, were all brought into being together. These things form, in fact, the Biblical definition of humanity at the moment of The Fall. In less Judeo-Christian-Islamic-Mormon terms, these things all share a single point of origin in ourselves.

Reading this, I sense a truth. Meditating on it, I discover evidence of truth. Testing it against my experience, I see it is true. Sex, it turns out, is central to what I see in myself and identify as human spirituality. It is, therefore, equally empowered to advance or retard my spiritual development. More sex may lead to a more spiritual life, or it may mitigate against my spiritual goals. Sex approached with more honesty and with an ecstasy-inclined inner adjustment can only lead to clearer spiritual vision. Any soul-to-soul contact between humans awakens spirit, and every degree of awakening is a boon to spiritual development.

Again, be warned, though I write with the pens of men and angels, I do not have the Pope's permission to tell you what is good or bad for your soul.

Am I supposed to stay present and accountable when I'm being flogged? Sometimes I try, but I can't. I drift away and miss what the Top is saying and doing (except for the flogging), then I feel foolish and wrong when my absence is discovered.

What you are supposed to do when you are being flogged is experience the flogging. If your experience of the flogging includes what you call drifting away, so be it. Now that you know this about yourself, tell the Tops who are going to flog you what to expect. The best of them will be glad to know, and may change the way they approach the flogging in order to facilitate rather than interfere with your experience. The most sensitive will even find ways to hitch a ride and drift with you to some extent.

If a Top demands that you remain present and take the flogging in a sense-alert condition, maybe he has his reasons. Perhaps you are drifting away too soon or too easily, so to speak, and traveling at a lower level than you might. A Top may also want you to stay with him to satisfy his sadism by wincing and yowling as he hurts you. If so, you may get to let go later in the scene, or not. Either way, you decide whether to afford him that pleasure, and he'll decide whether to book another play date.

In any case, any feeling that you are foolish or wrong is a mistake. There is nothing foolish about permitting yourself to respond naturally to sensation, nor is drifting away, as you call it, an inherently wrong way for a healthy person to deal with sensory stimulation.

Is it possible that I have out-of-body experiences when I'm tortured, or is there a more terrestrial explanation for the times when the pain stops being pain and the scene seems to be an "act" in slow motion?

To say that you have out-of-body experiences is one way of accurately and realistically describing a personal event that others might describe as seeing God, becoming God, or just getting really high. How such experiences are perceived and reported has to do with how a person is raised, what he expects, and what words he thinks will be acceptable to the person he is telling.

Regardless of the description, I have had such experiences and helped others achieve them as well. It can take hours of dissecting the experience and struggling with language for two people to see that one man's out-of-body experience is identical in form with another man's experience of being suddenly aware that his body is and contains the entire universe. The languages of all religions and faiths, cultures and contemporary sciences can be bent to describe such inner events, but none of them can express the essence of the experience to people who have not also "been there and done that."

If you are more comfortable with a "more terrestrial" explanation, you might appreciate the descriptions offered by biochemistry. It is my contention, however, that even if no language is better than any other for the purpose at hand, it still matters very much to each of us to be *heard* and understood when we describe our experiences in language that has meaning for us. What's more, no language provides anything more than a descriptive vocabulary. There are no words to explain what we "come back" knowing about ourselves. Description is not explanation, but it is all we have sometimes.

When I've been playing hard for a long time, I get a buzz. If the play goes on after that, I get high like I used to on drugs, without the after-effects. I'm pleased by all of this, and have not experienced any problem because of it. Still, I'm worried that I could be making poor or dangerous decisions when I'm in this state. What do you think?

I, too, used to worry that the high I arrived at by way of pain processing would be dangerous to my ability to make safe, sane judgments, especially about consent. This danger never materialized in all my years as a bottom, and I eventually dismissed my fears.

Since the mid-1980s I have done a lot of Topping, and my view has changed. I now know that there are people who get into a state where their judgment *is* severely impaired when they get a strong dose of naturally occurring opioids in their blood. When I find bottoms I know to be reasonable and of sound mind wriggling and shuddering and begging for activity I know would injure or kill them, I know what to do. I step up my vigilance, monitor every breath and twitch, and try to stimulate them in ways that will satisfy their need for more without injuring them.

If you discover (or have reason to suspect) that you enter involuntary states of this no-judgement sort during heavy scenes, select your Tops all the more carefully, and tell them what you can about it.

In my experience, it turns out that bottoms whose involuntary states are this extreme are not all that rare. Even in vanilla sex, I've heard "Slam it into me, tear me apart," and such. It stands to reason that more intense experience would lead to more intense expressions of the same kind. On the other hand, a very trustworthy Top—which is always a good thing to have around—is an absolute necessity if you suspect there may be moments when you cannot trust yourself. The other alternative—calling a halt to every scene before it gets you *there*—is unthinkable.

This answer, so far, has been composed with the assumption that the person "going involuntary" is the bottom. There is a more or less corresponding experience that is accessible to Tops. Of course, when a Top enters an "involuntary" state, it is essential that something otherwise not present should take control of the scene. I am hesitant to attempt any description of the condition I am mentioning, but I am willing to describe a scene in which this very special "event" occurred.

I arrived at a party of The 15 Association, in a fairly revved-up condition. I suppose a lot of that was due to a lengthy discussion of my favorite leather literature—*The Story of Harold*, *Ready to Catch Him Should He Fall*, *The Real Thing*, and *The Rose Exterminator*—since nothing gets me going like the reflection of intelligence on reality, particularly when that intelligence is focused on my reality. So, for the sake of literature, or whatever, I arrived in a *very* "ready to go" frame of mind, and had a date to flog Piglet (which, of course, may have had something to do with my excitement). I had also been working very hard, then suddenly having a restful day—another factor in creating the special effect to come, I suspect. In any case, it is necessary that you understand that I was in a state to expect something outstanding, or—more precisely—I was ready to have a very, very good time.

Eventually, Piglet and I found a place to play, and the flogging began. Our progress was fairly rapid, as we had less than two and a half hours before Piglet was due to put in his hour of work for the party. I won't bore you with the details of my selecting and using one whip after another, nor will I titillate you with the beauty of Piglet, bound to nothing more stable than himself, standing there absorbing the energy of the blows, extending himself toward me and toward the experience we both hoped for.

There came a moment when I was flogging Piglet with a braided cat held in my right hand, while reaching around him, holding him against my own body with a bow made of my left arm. This went on some few minutes, constantly increasing in intimacy and energy, then, in a split second, a world of thoughts arrived in my mind fully formed. How can I be holding Piglet and, at the same time, flogging him with such a long whip? Who's arm is *that*, reaching out to stroke my shoulder? Where can my feet be to be supporting me while all this is happening? Am I being flogged? Is Piglet really okay with what is happening? Does it matter that I don't know which is the floor and which the ceiling? Do up and down really mean two different things? Is it possible that I was once not part of this boy, this experience, this moment?

You have to believe me that no description will suffice to express my experience in this scene or any of the few that have also delivered me into the same condition. Guy Baldwin gave me a name for the experience a few weeks later at Leatherfest in San Diego. "That is called fusion," he said as I happened to mention the event during a discussion of advanced play. Having a name, knowing others had a similar experience, and setting the scene in a public way was good for me, perhaps even cathartic, but it didn't change the fact that the capital-T truth of the moment remained inexpressible.

This sort of involuntary experience is all that I find safe for a Top to permit himself. Why? Because I believe—from experienced deductions—that something I consider higher than my own best efforts is in control at times like these. I feel absolutely sure that a bottom who is safe with me in my usual watchful mode is doubly (or infinitely more) safe when this "other" intrudes.

I am having a spiritual crisis: I went out of my way to discover that the Bible doesn't condemn homosexuality—that God didn't, anyway, even if St. Paul did, and pretty weakly at that. Now, I'm into leathersex, and I'm worried that the same peace of mind is not accessible. It isn't, is it?

Well, if you can be satisfied by the discovery that the Bible doesn't condemn SM, relax. If you need to find the word of God expressly commanding you to go forth and beat the hell out of your partners and lovers, you're in trouble. I suppose there are preachers who would be able to twist a Bible verse here and a Christian injunction there to read as though they had something to do with SM, but a calmer view is easily achieved: the Bible says nothing about SM.

By the way, I'd call this a crisis of religion, not spirit. Religions codify rules that are intended to help people discover or adhere to practices that will support them in their spiritual lives. Being organizations, which is shorthand for oversized committees, religions are not very good at keeping up with the changes of conditions under which their financially supportive communities live. Spirit, by comparison, guides us in similar ways and with similar goals, but can never be out of date, not even by micro-seconds.

I know that you have lost at least two boys/slaves to AIDS, and I have heard that your first Top, your first relationship-bottom, and an early lover have also died. So, you have to be able to answer this question: How do you ever again start playing when you have had even one such loss? I think I can sort of understand how bottoms can get going again, but how can a Top?

I'm not all that sure it is any easier for bottoms than for Tops to resume leathersex after the death of a partner. I'm not even sure it is harder to resume leathersex than any other sort of sex, although it seems so to me.

To answer you in any general way is probably impossible, but I can tell you some of what has been helpful to me.

My slave scott died very slowly, wasting away for well over a year after the last time we were able to play, wearing me down and, at his death, leaving me with conflicting feelings of grief and relief. Playing with anyone seemed impossible. Before long I *wanted* to play, or at least to have sex, but I felt none of the confidence and energy I'd need for SM and little of the hard-dick spark I'd need for sex. I went to a few parties. At first, being at the parties was more frustrating than liberating since everyone seemed to feel that either I needed to play with them "to help me get over it" or they needed to help me feel better by not "pushing" me to play. Both attitudes left me uneasy. Eventually, it was not the help offered by friends but my own indomitable ego that carried the day. I'd see a flogging or an electrical scene, for instance, and think I could do it better. And, even if I should be embarrassed to admit it, those bursts of ego were just what I needed to get back into the fray. Notice, though, if I were not out among leathermen, exposing myself to the scene, this path would not have been open to me.

Two years later, warren died rather suddenly. There was no relief mingled with my grief. There was only the feeling that no one could ever be anywhere near as good to me or as good for me as warren had been. In other words, I was desperately lonely and very much lost in my feelings. Two months later I was scheduled to be at Chicago Hellfire Club's Inferno. I remembered how I'd used an arrogant version of monkey-see/monkey-do after scott's death, but I found myself avoiding the dungeons at Inferno. Then a boy named ben began insisting on my attention. I imagined that my friend Piglet had put him up to it for my sake, but he persisted longer than he'd have bothered if there were nothing else to it. He cleverly demanded only slight attentions at first, and very slight increases as the hours and days passed. The small steps, in the leathersex pressure cooker of the run, escalated rapidly into a scene.

So, once it was a weakness in my character that impelled me back to playing, and once I was, to put it crudely, seduced back onto the field. What the two have in common is that the opportunity to get back to playing grew out of choosing to expose myself to leathersex situations. There was no plan, no intentional technique either time. Maybe this is a subject we should be discussing openly at conferences and leatherfests around the country. Any useful information would surely be appreciated by an ever-growing percentage of the leathersex population.

For the last several months I've had no interest in leathersex at all. I still want to get off, but the slightest touch of rough stuff

just turns me off. Is this common? Am I turning into one of "them"?

Since you didn't mention any traumatic experience as the genesis of this change in your interest level, I'll assume there is no bad scene to be blamed or anything of that kind. That being the case, yes, it is common for leatherfolk to have periods of lesser or no interest in leather sexuality. Choosing not to play for a period of weeks or months is pretty usual, and I've known guys who just never got around to playing for a year or two then came back to it in their own time.

Jim, a friend of mine in Los Angeles, was so shocked when this happened to him that he scheduled appointments with a psychiatrist and a medical doctor. Both were willing to examine him and discuss his situation, and both came up with the same diagnosis: Nothing. The psychiatrist was more probing, discovering that Jim had also stopped drinking coffee for almost two years at an earlier time, but eventually went back to his six cups a day. "Same thing," he said, "and it doesn't even matter what the cause might have been." The medical doctor was very practical: "There may even be a physical or hormonal reason, but we could spend a fortune searching for it, doing science that has never been done before, with no promise that we'd ever find anything." Jim went to San Francisco for a Folsom Street Fair weekend about eight months later, met a big guy he liked, and missed the fair completely—back to his old habits.

Another friend (we'll call him Bozo!) was convinced when he lost interest in SM that all of leathersex had been just a phase he had gone through. He was over it, suddenly preaching his gospel of The Phase to everyone. His beautifully equipped dungeon and 10-year collection of toys was sold when he hadn't used them for two or three months. Another three months later he was trying to relocate and buy back the best of his toys.

The moral: Don't worry, and don't dispose of toys right away.

I've been a weekend leatherman for years, and I am not satisfied with that, but I can't think how to bring my leather lifestyle into my Monday through Friday lifetime. What can I do to feel these two lives are one?

The easy answers are useless, but if they aren't mentioned they'll be missed. If you could achieve your goal by either playing more often or getting into a relationship, you'd do it, wouldn't you? But probably more play or a relationship would fail to answer your needs anyway.

What is needed, I suspect, is a life in which *being* a leatherman has a meaning to you independent of scenes and sex and affairs. Like being Black or Jewish or Republican, being a leatherman can have meaning, and should, seven days a week. While I can't think of any way to instill the necessary cultural values in the leather population, I can tell you that any effort to achieve those values for yourself will be greatly rewarded in the intangible riches that added up to a good life, well-lived in the pursuit of happiness.

To help you understand what I am talking about, I submit the following editorial titled "Back to the Future, or Vice Versa," which I wrote for *Drummer* #159, the last issue I edited.

> Over the past few years I have been imploring every *Drummer* reader to do something—from each according to his ability—to help secure the civil rights of gay people, leatherfolk, and other sexual minorities. If, for the moment, I turn my attention away from that subject, despite a currently raging police war on us across the US and around the world, you must not think I have given up. Not a bit. We are still human and citizens of purportedly elected governments, and still due the full range of rights and protections our governments are constituted to defend and provide.

Nonetheless, it is time we looked a little closer to home, and did a thorough cleaning of a special sort. We need to re-establish the safety of local, national, and worldwide networking among leathermen, to reconfirm the values of honesty, integrity, and mutual protection, and to assert the importance of the brotherhood of leathermen.

Once upon a time, so recently that I was alive and sexual and new to the SM scene, the traditions of the gay male leather community were taut and invariable. To get in was an *achieved* recognition, to get to know the respected leaders of the community was an honor accorded by those closest to the leaders to those who had proven their seriousness and trustworthiness, and to advance in respect within the community was primarily a function of frank and honest dealings with the men of your leather/SM circle over time.

In the past 15 to 20 years, leathermen have become impatient with these slow-acting traditions. We have allowed our well-founded eagerness to be accepted by at least a certain range of the outside public to undo the carefully constructed separateness in which leather culture could rightly claim to be grounded in trust, integrity, and mutual acquaintance. We have let our taste for "fresh meat" (or, more generously, our willingness to share) overpower our need to monitor our own community and our need to be able to close ranks against those who (even if leather clad) are the enemies of our values. And perhaps worst of all, by rejecting our traditions, we have cast out of our community the elders we ought to revere.

The losses are immeasurable. All the negotiating of scenes, all the insuring of safety, all the tests of sanity, and all the constantly reasserted claims of consensuality can only—at best—echo the sense we once had of a safe, loving fraternity of like-minded men.

It all leaves me, on the one hand, nostalgic for the way things were. But I know that once a door is opened, it is not possible to close it and recapture an atmosphere that has blown away.

So, on the other hand, I am left wondering what can be done *now* to establish for the future a leather community with respectable values, with cultural habits that amount to cohesion and mutual support. I want our community to be a population which, by whatever means, is safe from dishonesty within and safer than the current one from "enemy" attacks.

What, I ask myself, could instill in leathermen again the high regard for honest interaction we once relied on so comfortably?

I don't know the answer to this question. You probably don't either. In fact, if anyone has a workable answer, he is probably to be found among the leathermen over 65 who are so cruelly marginalized in our rush-to-the-future present culture. The answer, or at least the part of it we're most sorely lacking today, must have to do with how the strict value systems of the original leather community were established in the 1940s and `50s when proud SM players, tired of at-your-own-risk encounters, invented the modern leather/SM/fetish world view.

Getting a value-honoring, honesty-valuing leather community going again is something I'm ready to work on, something I'm willing to live for. How about you? I'd really like to hear/read your thoughts and feelings and plans.

If we can achieve this move forward into a future that recaptures what was most valuable in our past, we will be all the more prepared to stand up in reliable numbers for our rights in the larger world. We will be more able to depend on one another for the mutual support that makes a group a community. We will be more ready to incorporate and appreciate new ideas, new people, and the new pressures the future will deliver into our community.

10

LEATHERSEX PAST

I hesitate to quote here the old saw about those who don't learn from the past being doomed to repeat it. That's meant to warn people that what was *not* good in the past will haunt the future if its lessons are not learned and taught. The problem in the leather lifestyles is a little different. We run the risk of suffering from failing to retrieve what *was* good in our past. Granted, the questions here run at a slight bias to this theme, but I had to take this chance to say my piece.

An older leatherman once said to me, "The first rule used to be 'don't scare the townsfolk,' now it's 'get yours and damn anyone who gets in the way'." I can make guesses of my own, but can you tell me what he meant?

By telling you a bit of my personal history, I think I can give you a good feel for the meaning of the now-antique line about the townsfolk.

In the 1960s I often went out with my Hollywood friends on

one or two weeknights, usually including Friday. We all wore makeup and flamboyant clothes, a mix of pieces we bought at the trendy men's shops and pieces found at The Playmate Shop or Frederick's of Hollywood. It was the only way I knew to be gay at the time, with the crowd I had fallen into by way of bus stations and movie theaters. In this circle, it was widely believed (and possibly true) that we had to be wearing at least three items of men's clothing in order not to be illegally cross-dressed. We often wore two pairs of socks to be extra safe since we were led to believe that shoes didn't count.

On two Saturdays a month I was at SM parties, many of which extended to or resumed at Sunday brunches. Come Saturday, I scrubbed away all traces of cosmetics and perfumes, and switched from fishnet bellbottoms to skin-tight blue jeans, from flouncy pirate shirts to plain pocket T-shirts.

My Hollywood friends at La Pergola on The Boulevard would squeal if a leatherman or even a Levi-clad butch hustler passed by the window. They wanted men like that, but they always disparaged every passerby through the protective glass: “Get her. Doesn't she even know she's queer as a purple giraffe?”

My weekend buddies, on the rare occasions when I was with any of them outside the dungeon apartment, were no more enlightened. “Filth!” they would hiss, looking at the likes of my weeknight friends, “Do they think gay men want women? Are they trying to *be* women?”

I didn't feel particularly torn between the two groups. If I wanted to have sex, it seemed obvious that the way to get it was in the Hollywood fashion, and I got plenty. If I wanted SM, I had no option but to butch it up with the weekend crowd. I thought of gay as the weekday mode, and male as the weekend mode, and was perfectly comfortable with the arrangement.

I often heard the comment “Don't scare the natives” or “Don't scare the townsfolk” among my SM pals, primarily as a reminder among themselves not to camp or otherwise appear gay in public.

Sometimes I felt a twinge of guilt, imagining what my SM friends would think if they saw me on a Friday, but I also saw a practical side to their thinking. The queens in drag and half-drag were being rolled, bashed, and sometimes killed. As far as I knew, no one who did that sort of thing would guess that we, in our butch drag, were gay or otherwise targets for their brutal attention.

I assume the remark had roots that went deeper. After all, the politics and conventions of the SM crowd were very military and extremely conservative, as far as I—aged 17 to 19—could tell. The politics of the queens, on the other hand, were about the oppression they faced on the sidewalks and streets, and there was more fighting back than laying back involved by 1966. There may be a practical source to be traced for each of these attitudes and the lifestyles that went with them, but I am not a sociologist so I'll take just one short stab at it: Most of my SM friends were either veterans or friends of veterans with actual military experience of discipline. Most of my openly gay friends were 4Fs, unwilling or unable to play straight long enough to get into the armed forces. So, the SM men often had veteran's benefits to protect, the queens had nothing to lose in that way.

Before I go on, I should point out one other thing that may seem strange but is probably relevant to my understanding of the attitude embodied in "Don't scare the townsfolk." I didn't know during the first year or more of my involvement with the SM group that the leatherboys (we called them boys, not men) were in any way related to the SM men. So, in my SM circle, the leatherboys were thought to be scaring the townsfolk as much as the drag queens were. This led to more than a little confusion when I eventually made the connection between leather chaps and whips, but that came later. My history with that first circle of SM players made it very hard for me to get into actually wearing leather on the street. Like many of my friends, as late as 1970, I was carrying my leathers to the bar, dressing inside or at the car, then changing back to "street clothes" for the trip home.

Over time, the politics of various gay factions coalesced somewhat. Drag and leather and vanilla gays, muscle hunks and chubbies, as well as racially different populations learned some measure of cooperation. Meantime, I learned I didn't have to have a hand in every gay world to get laid the way I wanted to.

After a variety of uprisings—usually symbolized by the otherwise unremarkable Stonewall Resistance—open expressions of gay pride became common. During this time of realignment leather and SM men seemed to be very important in organizing things, but less visible when it came time to step out publicly, probably another effect of the veteran's benefits to be protected, or just inertia. Besides, to many older men who had apprenticed in the secretive society of 1950s and `60s gay SM, the publicity was appalling. To the SM men, everything gay men were doing in this then-new age of activism smacked of flaunting, inviting reprisal, and impropriety.

To this day, and I am sure for a very long time to come, the reality of these two points of view reverberates loudly in the gay community. On the one side we have the adherents of the "Don't scare the townsfolk" philosophy. They read and appreciate assimilationist books like *After the Ball*, and they either don't support the efforts of the gay rights movement or they try to do so only "within the system," usually by sending checks to lobbying groups. On the other side we have Act Up and the grand gestures of gay pride parades. This side has plenty of literature and a very loud voice.

There is, of course, a majority of the gay community which falls between the two extremes. It seems your older friend has not adjusted to the middle ground of the 1990s. I wonder if I ever shall really get there myself.

My first leather lover/Top told me there were a lot of regulations, and made me follow his version of them, but now he's gone and I feel lonely—no one else knows or follows those

rules. Or, maybe I'm looking in all the wrong places.

There were *a lot* of regulations in the circles that nurtured me through my early years in leathersex. I alternately resisted and relied on these regulations. I rebelled, usually in silence, at one moment and reveled the next moment in the simple certainty of knowing *my place*.

Through the 1970s, I watched as bathhouse conventions supplanted the traditional constraints of leathermen. Through the 1980s, I was stunned to hear the very men who had overturned the prescriptive regimentation of leather ways in favor of 18 butt holes or cocks or fists or floggers in a weekend, suddenly blaming each other for not keeping the light of leather customs lit and attended. And, in the 1990s, I am finding more and more people—most of them too young to know—wondering if such a noble lifestyle as the Old Guard of Leather ever really existed. I sometimes even find myself wondering if the glittering of the before-time in my mind is more nostalgia than genuine memory.

But, yes! We did live differently once. Our biases and limitations may have been abhorrent, but no one ever threw out a more promising baby with such slightly soiled bath water before.

The good news is that there are still old guys who remember, there are still young fellows who desire, and there are many people like yourself who have an understanding of what we are lacking today. The last question in Chapter 9 is pretty closely related to yours, and despite the long answer I've given you here, you may find something relevant in that as well.

So, you probably *can* find men as eager to live with the regulations as you are, but you'll have to find a way of letting people know you're looking for what most folk today would call an Old Guard relationship. Further good news: Couples who publicly observe traditional leather conventions today are more numerous than they were five years ago, and they are not ignored as they were in 1980 or ridiculed as they were in 1987. Instead, they are usually noticed with respect, even reverence, and treated with deference. To these old eyes, that looks like progress.

Is the Old Guard still around? I think I need it.

See the answer above, and brace yourself for a long hard search to find a way in. The now-widening circle of traditional leathermen is understandably nervous about newcomers.

Is there really an esoteric leathersex tradition as in *The Real Thing* and *The Quest*?

The esoteric leather traditions of *The Real Thing* and *The Quest* are two very different things, but not entirely unrelated. If you are waiting for the magical moment when your performance in SM is so perfect and honest and honorable that a godlike Maestro of human affairs blesses you with an invitation to the Absolute Elite of Leathersex, keep dreaming and striving. There may be no Leather Valhalla or SM Elysium but there is the inexpressible joy of being noticed and accepted by the leathermen you most respect. There is also a genuine elite corps of algolagniac gourmets who, given a taste of your skills, may invite you to their feasts.

Or, maybe I'm wrong. Maybe I am simply unable to see what I cannot personally achieve. Maybe there really is an association of demigods and gods of leather sexuality. I won't be surprised to find that it's true. After all, anything can happen on this planet!

I've been going from relationship to relationship for 18 years. Now, for the first time, I'm on my own. The leather world has changed while I was being kept busy. Can you help me catch up?

Eighteen years ago it was 1977. The most startling changes in the leather world since then are the broadening of the world encompassed by the word *leather* and a tremendous boom in publishing.

Today there are leather drag queens—Tops and bottoms—and leather faeries, too. There are leathermen who never wear leather, and leathermen who always wear rubber or spandex or neoprene. And what wouldn't have been believed in 1977 is that all the various leather styles can and do get along pretty well most of the time. Leather nudists and leather purists party and share bars with leather faeries and leather novices. Harley riders and Honda bikers may still fuss at each other, but I haven't heard of road hogs spilling rice burners (Harley riders forcing riders of Japanese bikes off the road) for at least 15 years. Leathermen and leatherwomen, gay, straight and bisexual sometimes play together these days, and can usually share public space in peace and work together on fundraisers and shows.

As for the publishing I mentioned, in 1977 my leather library was kept in a thin canvas valise in a two-inch space between the head of my bed and the wall. Larry Townsend's *Leatherman's Handbook*, in its third printing, was still more or less alone as the representation of leather lit with any but a jack-off purpose. In 1995, my leather library, at about 225 books, is small by comparison to many others I have seen. And, in 1977, *Drummer* was still pretty new, undiscovered by most leathermen, and almost completely alone on the few magazine racks willing to stock it. Today, the number of leather/SM/kinky periodicals is staggering, and new ones show up almost every month.

If you want to catch up on the last couple of decades, read during the daylight hours, and party at night, but be ready to live in a brave new world that has such creatures in it as the male dominatrix and the female boy-slave, the non-SM Bear and his cub, the pagan and wiccan leather ritualists, and lots of bored, upwardly mobile, weekend leathermen.

Oh, and the wild SM sex clubs of San Francisco, the ones you remember from 1977, they're all gone. We do those intense scenes at organized parties now, under the watchful eyes of Dungeon Masters, but *we still do everything we ever did and more.*

I had the dream of getting Etienne to draw my fantasy. This is a service he advertised. Now, he's gone. Is there anyone left who can do this sort of thing?

Custom fantasy art works are often an important part of an erotic artist's income. Perhaps the artists with high concepts to explore and important themes to express don't take such commissions, but most of us (yes, including me) do commissioned scenes.

Often the price of a custom work can be very high, but it can sometimes be partially offset if you permit the artist to also use the piece as a magazine illustration or on greeting cards or to offer it to other buyers in the form of a print. And some artists will create your custom art work for a relatively low fee if you will be satisfied with a signed print, allowing them to show the original in an exhibition where they can hope to earn a higher price for it.

I know that Dade-Ursus, The Hun, and Matt accept commissions. Dade specializes in Bears and does body hair and sleaze very handsomely, especially in his newly-evolved hard-line ink drawing style. The Hun is too well known to need a descriptive introduction, but I'd certainly go to him for great muscles, black men, and engorged exaggerations. Matt, who actually advertises for fantasy commissions, is the absolute king of wrestling scenes on paper and, I am told, in life. I do silhouettes.

Many cartoonists in the leather community are also willing to turn out specialty panels.

Shop the available art skills and styles by looking at magazines and book covers reflective of your fantasy. When you see an artist whose work would do, check for ads placed by the artist in magazines (often the same magazine where the illustration appears). Besides the display ads, artists often are found in the commercial classified ads. If there are no ads to give you the artist's address, write to the artist in care of the editor of the magazine or publisher of the book.

Don't expect an artist to work for nothing. It is impossible to tell you what it will cost to have a custom fantasy drawn or painted or, in my case, cut out of paper. The artist's popularity, the medium he works in, the number of figures required in your fantasy, the amount of background you want, and the complexity of the clothing, hair, and equipment can all figure into the final price, especially as they add to the time the artist will have to spend on your fantasy.

Rest assured that even if Etienne was the grand master of a certain style, his influence is still very much alive today. So, Etienne-like drawings are still available, as are many, many other styles, including one or more that you will like.

Was Tom of Finland a leatherman? I mean, did he do SM and leathersex, or just fantasize about it and draw pictures?

I didn't know Tom, although I did have the opportunity to talk to him once.

Tom was a leather god! I hear rumors of his vanilla-hood from time to time, and I shudder to think people might believe them. He talked very comfortably about leathersex and fetishism (uniforms never ceased to fascinate him) as a man who had explored these things personally and passionately.

I believe myself to be a man with good radar for detecting phonies, even among the idols of the community, and my screen never showed a single blip as Tom spoke of boots, uniforms, whipping, or bondage. Let the gossip die here: Tom was one of us.

I've been doing SM since the early 70s, so it seems I ought to be pretty used to all of it, but I can't get used to guys in skirts and women's underwear at all-male play parties. If I understood

what they're doing would I find it any easier to live with?

If you understood what they are doing you'd probably run from them, screaming and tearing your hair out. After all, nothing is more ridiculous than someone else's intimate reality. Are you in the starting blocks now? They're doing leathersex their way! The guys who do gender play so openly today are usually not engaged in games of femininity as humiliation at all. Instead, they are either investigating gender roles or, having done so, are playing in the roles that they find comfortable and expressive of something in themselves.

I know one young man who takes great pleasure in strutting around in lingerie, then performing regally as a pain scene Top. He admits that part of the joy for him is derived from the consternation he evokes in more traditional leathermen, but he still does his strut-and-strike show even when no one will be surprised by it.

Other leathersex players like to toy with their own gender appearance as a way of working internal buttons and levers to keep themselves a little bit off balance. These guys are usually angling for a scene in which they will bottom, often to another player who is gender bending to some degree.

Still other leathermen are thoughtfully and carefully calling on their own feminine sides to witness and even monitor their leathersex performance. The deepest understanding of this is probably only accessible to others who share their spiritual goals.

My own point of view may be of little help to you, but I think the shocking appearance of a less than strictly masculine costume—especially in conjunction with matching behavior—often adds a needed element to a play party's energy. This is particularly true when gay leathermen are sharing space with women and straight couples. The gender-bending gay males, in a sense, buffer or bridge the differences. On the other hand, I also enjoy the power that can be generated at a party that is men only, male image only, masculinity-as-focus, with the leather-uniform dress code enforced.

For me, leathersex is a balancing act *on one level*. I live in an often emasculating world, not because of women but because of restrictions and laws and the fact that there is so much beyond any hope of control. Ultra-masculinity, then, is a remedy more often than it is a symptom of illness in my experience. But we are each living in and responding to differently perceived worlds. Baby Jane, the whip-wielding super Top, is often welcome in my world.

Why do leathermen wear leather? I understand leather whips and maybe even leather restraints, but why the clothes?

Would you believe we wear leather because we want to? Not enough, eh? We wear leather because the respected players before us did so, and the guys we hope to go home with tonight expect it of us. Still not enough? Would it help if I added arguments about auras, scents, fetishes, hardness, darkness, smoothness, the sound of a slap against tight fitting leather, the protection leather provides when you're on a motorcycle, and the way leather can equally hide or reveal the wearer's body?

If nothing there catches your fancy, I don't think a spiel about the historical or etiological perspectives will do it for you either, so I'll give you a brief and purely personal response.

I don't often wear much leather, but when I do I feel more sexual and sexier. I see myself as a darker and more formidable figure. I sense in myself a prowess which is not coming from my usual personality, but is being called up from my depths by the connection, through wearing leather, to the whole historic and present fraternity of leathermen. For me, leather acquires these special powers from images of my father in G.I. leathers on his 1949 Indian motorcycle and from images of leather-clad men who left me weak in the knees by acts as simple as *not* looking at me at the Ram's Head bar in Silverlake (Los Angeles, circa 1968).

I could explain leather clothing away, but I prefer to give in to the mystery. If you aren't caught up in the mystery yourself, don't feel compelled to buy or wear leather. Leather expresses not a fashion requirement, but an unresisted desire.

All the "gay genius" books have got me wondering if there were ever any famous men into SM. Do you know of any?

I know those gay genius books too. I remember a book actually titled *Gay Geniuses* which I read several times back in the Dark Ages. Of course, if any of the gay people mentioned then were into leathersex, no evidence of it was given in such books. Kinkiness in a subject being celebrated *despite his gayness* might have undermined the purpose of such books, and the authors were hardly likely to discover it anyway.

Still, the answer to your question is that there have been lots of leatherfolk, gay and otherwise, who have made their mark on history. No doubt, in fact, the number of famous people into SM is very similar, on a per capita basis, to the number of not-so-famous people into SM. The desire for leathersex is not a drive that responds to fame by either appearing under the pressure of the limelight or disappearing under public scrutiny. Now, on the other hand, any kind of sex, especially any kind of kink, is going to be more often discussed if only in whispers, more defensively denied, and more readily dismissed with regard to most famous people. Famous people, especially in the age of tabloid journalism, are highly likely to find it useful to disavow any involvement in non-missionary sex, if only because it diverts attention away from the subject of the person's fame.

I'm not really answering your question yet, am I? The answer is that there have been quite a few famous people about whom tales of kinky sex have been told which, under any kind of examination, must be considered true (at least by me).

Because I understand that having an answer to this question can be very important to the construction of good self-images among kinky folks, it seems appropriate to devote a bit of time and space to giving a good answer, even if it can, by no means, be a complete one.

Here is a tiny excerpt from an uncompiled, imaginary catalog of the famous kinky people I can think of. Many of these people were heterosexual, most were said to be bisexual, some were exclusively gay:

The heroic statue at the entrance to my mental pantheon of leather is that of (T. E.) Lawrence of Arabia, whose family never made more than the weakest public attempts to deny or disprove the stories circulating about his masochism. Recently, in fact, I saw Lawrence's brother, in a television interview (on A&E's "Biography") discussing the fact that he knew "immediately after his death but not before" of Lawrence's male-male floggings and birchings. Looming nearly as large, primarily because his life is so much more recent, is Michel Foucault, who leather-outed himself. Then there's Dag Hammerskjold, whose heirs have gladly mounted lawsuits to keep his name clear of any such imputation. He seemed to describe pretty clearly in his diaries both urges and actions which can only be understood if we accept that he was also a masochist. Madonna has made a fortune parading the fact of her kinkiness. And fashion made any number of late Victorian poets and artists uncareful about hiding their kinks so we know that many of them—like Lawrence—were members of flogging clubs in London (or so the news of the day would lead us to believe).

I don't suppose mentioning people who trained their talents along leather by-ways really adds much to this discussion, so those who are famous as leathermen—like Tom of Finland and Etienne—may be meaningless. However, people somehow seem to miss the fact that Robert Mapplethorpe was not just outrageously sexual, but loudly leathersexual. Similarly, the fuss about tycoon Malcolm Forbes's motorcycle collection usually obscures the tandem tales of his SM involvement.

Among those still closeted, if only thinly, there is a famous

Broadway composer/lyricist today who is secretly a leather Master, and I am told both serious and good at it. One West Coast composer spent a brief time under slave contract to a friend of mine, but chose to appear to the world as "a lifelong bachelor" and ended the relationship to achieve that lonely status. I know of at least three famous painters who, although known to be gay, have chosen not to expose anything further about their sex lives to public scrutiny. Two are gay leather Tops, one is actually a bisexual bottom (who prefers to be thought gay publicly). I could go on, but nameless lists of the living famous are little help, and are likely to become sources for rumor or worse.

Those supposedly documented as foot fetishists include Egyptian Queens Cleopatra and Hatshepsut, poets Charles Baudelaire, Hafiz, and Ovid, movie maker D. W. Griffith, philosopher Wolfgang von Goethe, Italian King Victor Emmanuel II, and author George du Maurier. This list, which I believe I could extend with a few minutes research, is based on a single chapter in William A. Rossi's *The Sex Life of the Foot and Shoe* (Routledge & Kegan Paul, 1977).

By examining the biographies of people known to be kinky, it would be fairly easy to sniff out other likely candidates. Then by cross-referencing and reading less obvious and less accessible texts, it would probably be possible to come up with a fairly extensive list of people who definitely were, probably were, and might have been involved in leathersex of one sort or another. Anyone undertaking this research would want to give great attention to the biographies (or autobiographies) written by close friends who were not themselves famous. And given the less ferocious laws that protect the reputations of the dead, it might be wise to give special attention to diaries, books written after the famous figure's death, and case records eventually released from medical sources, in the rare cases where they ever are. (I think we have discovered here another book that needs an author.)

On a related note, there is a question I find far more interesting than who had one foot in the history books and the other in the dungeon: How many people with great deeds in their futures, with great contributions to make to the course of human progress, with great ideas that might have comforted us or reshaped our lives, have remained in the shadows, never putting forward their heroic ideas or actions because they feared the scrutiny their leathersex lives would attract? I know of at least one very famous man, a businessman with a strong presence in the national government of his country, who felt that his hetero-leathersex life was such a potential bomb that he kept it under wraps as long as he could, then made arrangements to disengage from his own businesses and from all government duties before submitting completely to his Mistress, who had *all along* promised to remain as invisible "as a mole on a President's ass." This man was no Einstein or Churchill. At least, I didn't sense in him that level of greatness struggling to break free. Nonetheless, the facts of his life got me to thinking: What might I have done? What might some of my brilliant friends have done if they were not accommodating the prudery and bigotry of our time by either suppressing their actual urges or juggling dual lives, or far worse, giving up what they might have done in the world in favor of what they could not avoid doing in their sex lives?

Prudery kills. In the long run, in fact, the prudery of our age may be the greatest damper on our progress. Who knows what we are losing from the pool of human thinking and human achievement by the fact that we live in a world where prudery is a greater force than genius. Anyone who doubts that genius can be stifled need look no further than the now-famous case of Alan Turing and as far as we know he was just gay.

Where did the idea of using safewords come from?

There certainly is something murky about the origin of safewords, as such, and it may be that all or many of the theories that are advanced about them are true. It may just as well be true that all or many of them are false. I don't really know the whole story, but I am glad to contribute what I know to be true: As early as 1964, when I first began playing at parties in Los Angeles, there was something like a safeword policy in effect for the parties. Every bottom was told the name of the "host" (what we might call a dungeon master today) and was told that if he were in any kind of trouble, particularly with a Top who wouldn't take no for an answer, all he had to do was shout out the host's name. The scene would be stopped immediately by the host, and the bottom would be asked to leave immediately. In the only case of the use of this sort of "safeword" at one of the parties—the only one I know about in any detail—as soon as the bottom had cried out, he was released and told to leave immediately. Then all Tops available at the moment were convened in another room where within five minutes they decided to expel the Top. The bottom was called and told that he was welcome to come to future parties if he would first meet with the host privately at a certain time. The Top was never permitted to return.

This is the only kind of safeword I was familiar with until 1986, meaning I knew nothing of safewords being used in private, one-on-one scenes. In 1986, I heard about the idea of red-yellow-green words (which I still find humorous and even destructive of the power exchange and leathersex dynamic) from a dyke who thought every serious player already knew that these particular safewords were "standard."

Since that time they have become more and more common pretty much everywhere, and I have even instituted a kind of safeword that is permitted to be used in private scenes in my playroom. That is, I have reverted to my own earliest leathersex history: I tell bottoms that they are not, under any circumstances, to speak my name; if I hear my name, the scene is over. Otherwise, if something is wrong for them, they are expected to find a way to let me know without using my name. In the latter situation, they may be able to focus my attention on what they think I need to know without ending the scene.

11

LEATHERSEX MISCELLANY

Some questions just refuse to be categorized, no matter how loose and general you make the categories. These are the few that couldn't be forced into any other chapter, but neither could they be left out of the book.

I have a drawer full of pictures of my leathersex exploits. The problem is the film is all (all 100+ rolls of it) undeveloped. What can I do in Utah? And don't tell me to settle for fuzzy Polaroids. I can't do that.

[Note: When this question arrived, I was able to locate a willing photo lab in Salt Lake City with just three phone calls, not to labs, but to friends who would also use the services of such labs. The name and number of the lab was sent to the writer of the question immediately, and he rewarded me with a few very enjoyable pictures from his collection. Putting the name of a particular lab in this book would be inappropriate, especially since laws about the lab's liability in obscenity charges vary wildly from place to place and time to time, and most particularly since doing such business in the U.S. mails can so easily lead to prosecution.]

Wherever you are, you need to be somewhat careful with your explicit photography. For one thing, even the most reputable labs will sometimes (not *all* of them, *maybe*) make prints of your pictures for private use. This might not be such a terrible price to pay if we could be sure that they would remain completely private, but any prints other than your own are invasions of your privacy. A couple of years ago, I inherited a series of photo albums, pictures duplicated from customer film and collected by a man who worked in a San Francisco franchise of a major photo lab chain. He had collected separate albums of fisting and double-fisting, nude muscle boys posing outdoors, scat scenes, blood sports, and an amazing array of household items being forced into body cavities.

These extra prints are the lesser of the three major problems. The greater problem is in the area of arrest and prosecution based on the evidence of your film, and this process can just as well start from the confiscation of the extra prints as from your own. A single "civic-minded citizen" working in a lab can turn your photos into convincing evidence against you.

Between the more or less innocuous collecting of extra prints and the extreme of legal action, is the middling disappointment of having your film returned to you processed and destroyed rather than processed and printed. Some labs, when they notice explicit sexual images, will bleach, mark, or punch out the offensive segments of each negative. I have heard of this happening in New York, Chicago, San Francisco, and Dallas, so I assume it could happen anywhere. And, even if this destruction of your property were illegal, it would be dangerous to attempt prosecution. (The reason it is not illegal is that labs offer, in the event that your film is destroyed or lost, nothing more than replacement of the film, and you effectively accept this policy when you hand your film in.)

So, trust referrals. Asking the lab if it's willing to process and print extreme erotic images may or may not get you an honest and reliable answer. In the absence of reliable *local* referrals, shop farther from home. While labs that offer uncensored processing by mail in the classified ads of gay and leathersex magazines are not necessarily free of problems (extra prints especially), they are probably safe from legal hassles and the destruction of your film, especially if their ads have been running for a long time.

Safe, uncensored service either by mail or in an area where such service is rare will very likely cost more than regular photo processing. You can often reduce the cost significantly by carrying your film in and picking it up even from labs that do mail order business as well. Save up between vacations or whatever, and avoid the shipping and handling charges that mount up astronomically with some labs, and you'll avoid the possibility that your pictures will be seized in the mail at the same time.

Do you know of any place at all where it is okay to do heavy scenes outdoors?

Outdoor scenes are never sure to remain private and undisturbed unless you or someone you know owns the land and intentionally secures it. The other real options, obviously, are the few SM runs that include outdoor scene space, like The 15 Association's Bootcamp each June and Chicago Hellfire Club's Inferno each September. There are actually at least a few other sunlit dungeon runs every year, but generally if you are welcome, you'll hear about them.

Doing scenes on public land can work. It has for me anyway. A lot of planning and hiking and risk-reduction preparations are required, but the pleasures are worth the efforts. I have used (but never will again after mentioning them in a book) the oasis at Chinaman Wells out from Las Vegas, high ridges above the Russian River in Northern California, hike-in areas of the Mojave desert, a remote area of the lower mesa on the Navajo reservation in New Mexico, and a battered ghost town on Indian land out from Palm Springs.

You can find places, believe me, but it isn't easy. If you know a local nudist/naturist group, especially a gay one, you might find some help there. If you know any members of off-road biking groups, they often know both where to go and when.

So, the places I've found are places that have worked for me, but you—being in a different part of the country, and hoping for a different kind of scene—will need to work up a list of your own.

People often talk about what width of a butt strap is the legal minimum for the street, whether handcuffs, saps, weapons, or bull-dog spikes can be visible (legally) in public, etc. How do I find out the facts about the law and my lifestyle?

There has been a lot of discussion of this subject over the years, and a sudden flurry of postings about it on the Internet as I write this chapter (February, 1995). The consensus seems always to come down to this: We *can't* get reliable answers. There seems to be a powerful call for a book on the subject, but everyone recognizes that such a book would become dated on its way to the printer. Nonetheless, a lawyer or university law class could give us something of at least general usefulness if they were willing to undertake the massive amount of research involved.

From time to time, I've been at leather events where part of the registration package was a list of relevant local laws, mainly concerning how little one can legally wear in public. Law columns in magazines don't seem to last very long, and the advice is usually advice rather than actual statements about what laws are on the books and how they are interpreted and enforced.

In an attempt to zero in on something specific here, I called a Southern California lawyer. His remarks—again, in the category of advice—are not very detailed: "If you're questioning any item of clothing or public action, treat it as though it is illegal and you're probably safe." Maybe we don't want to be safe by erring constantly on the side of caution. Besides, what if we don't question our right to wear handcuffs on our belts (illegal in many states and cities) or to carry a whip onto an airplane (a matter left to airport security and usually not a problem). I need the facts as much as anyone, and don't seem to have any better access to the information I need than you do.

My best hope of an answer for any given question relevant to any given time and place is to ask direct questions of the people who have recently produced leather events in the area. Even these people usually have only guesses and warnings to offer. Understanding that state regulations are sometimes interpreted loosely or made more stringent by counties, parishes and cities, you'll want the most recent and most local information you can get. I suspect that the eventual answer to all of this will be some kind of constantly updated database on the Internet. This would allow people who know to list the existing laws, change the listings as the laws change, report about how the laws are being enforced, and how the local community deals with the laws.

I get the feeling that leathersex attracts only intelligent, reasonable, and generally kind men. Does it seem that way to you too?

I get that feeling sometimes myself, but then I run into one or more of the people I find I can't approve of. It would be so comforting to be able to dismiss these guys with some brush of the mental hand that simply suggests they aren't really part of the leather community. However, if there is really a leather community in this country or the world, I have to admit there are idiots in it, and people who are just not to my liking, and even people I have to consider criminal. There are men who, under current social and cultural conditions, have to be called leathermen, even though they are not people I trust or want to have in my life.

And still, the feeling comes back over and over again. Time after time, in one situation after another, I find myself way more than half willing to agree with your assessment of the leathersex population. You should know, by the way, that I hear this question often. So, I comfort myself with the knowledge that my own network of lovers and playmates and friends and acquaintances is full to bursting with people I approve of wholeheartedly. The result of this view of the leather world is that I believe a trustworthy man or woman becomes surrounded by others like himself or herself. A person who cares and "gets it" has a life, in this community, full of people who care and "get it" too.

I don't think heterosexuals are quite as lucky in this regard, and I know most gay men are far less fortunate. It's just one more way that I find myself appreciating and even loving the leather community. (I am resisting an urge to start listing the wonderful people I know and have known in three decades of leathersex, but I know the names are not at issue.) We are a good lot, and I don't think it hurts to stop very, very briefly now and then and pat ourselves on the back.

I don't have room to build a dungeon, but I really want a space that's all for leathersex. Has anyone written a book or anything about having convertible equipment or a concealable dungeon in regular living space?

The book you are looking for doesn't exist as far as I know, but many of its chapters have been published in *DungeonMaster* over the years, and one or two have turned up in *Sandmutopia Guardian.* Like the book on SM and the law, this is one I believe a lot of people are waiting for, but not *as many* since this volume would be a how-to for only those willing to take up the saw and hammer, and go to work.

There are a handful of dungeon carpenters out there who have become very clever about the kind of construction you need, but it gets very expensive. Ask around—these few builders are pretty evenly scattered around the country. Meantime, get the old *DungeonMasters* whether you are planning to do your own building or hire someone to do it.

I feel like I need to be giving something back to the leathermen in my community. I'm not rich, but I have a decent income and some free time, as well as a lot of grateful energy. Problem is, I don't have the kind of face or body that gets elected Mr. Anything in leather. What would you suggest?

What each of us can do, and how much we can do to promote the comfort, happiness, convenience, and security of the leather community, depends almost not at all on how well we are equipped to perform in leather contests or as titleholders. Indeed, those of us who never hold or compete for titles are more free in a way to serve the needs of the community. Since we are devoting no energy to preparing for one or more attempts to become titleholders, and since we are not living with expectations and reputations connected to titles, we can look for needs at any time and do what we can to meet them. This is not to say that people without titles are necessarily better or more active in leather community service, but we are far more numerous. No way around it, regardless of the ever-changing qualities and abilities of titleholders, the armies of ordinary mortals they represent will always do most of the work, provide most of the service, kick in or collect most of the money needed by the community. The benefits of being a titleholder can be desirable, but they are also easily susceptible to overestimation. Still, it has to be understood that *not* having a title is no impediment to active and effective involvement in and service to the leather community.

Perhaps I can be forgiven if I take advantage of this one serious question to pontificate a bit on related subjects. In fact, I had considered a chapter—perhaps as many as 30 questions and answers—about titles, titleholders, contests, and the service-to-enjoyment ratio of community involvement. Because the questions overlap so deeply, and because one organized answer seems to make more sense that 30 fragments, I prefer to answer all the questions together.

What the title system does for the community, in effect, is very good. By drawing together people from all over the country and around the world, events like International Mister Leather, International Mister Drummer, and Living in Leather (with Mr. and Ms. NLA: International) give us an opportunity to share experiences, communicate between local groups, develop and maintain friendships, and to offer each other emotional and practical support in times of crisis and change, even when the relevant needs are more or less local in nature. That means that the title system—or at least its contest events—provides not just a *sense* of community, but the very structure of the community. In the 1990s, the title contest events are more popular, and therefore more effective, than motorcycle runs, community awards programs, or other similar types of events.

There are many other elements of our community's structure. Magazines like *Drummer*, *The Leather Journal*, *International Leatherman*, and *DungeonMaster/Checkmate*; books like this one and the many other nonfiction titles being published each year; and events sponsored by leather/SM/fetish clubs around the country all have contributions to make to defining, refining, and upholding our community. All of these also offer opportunities for individuals to participate in the making and maintaining of the community. What's more, every possible major contributor to the community on a large scale has cognates on every scale. If there are a handful of international title contests, there are several dozen regional, and several hundred local contests. The few national and international magazines are met on the regional and local levels by, again, dozens or hundreds of smaller publications. And, while you could count on the fingers of one hand the Infernos and Bootcamps and other internationally significant club-sponsored events, you can find events every weekend all across the country, which are the same but for their scale.

The supremacy of the title contests is not a pure value judgement. It is an organic fact *at this time*. The title contests hold their positions of importance in the overall community in three ways: They provide the largest number of people with opportunities for actual, face-to-face, skin-to-skin, and mind-to-mind contacts and exchanges. They are able to influence and to reflect influence from the community more rapidly and more powerfully than other events because they combine so many diverse elements of social, sexual, cultural, and political interaction. And, finally, they provide (at their best) spokespersons who are chosen because they represent what is of significance in the community at the time, meaning these titleholders (again, the good ones only) are able to carry the current messages of identity and intention from point to point throughout the community. This final idea is supported by the attention titleholders get at events, in magazines, and in person-to-person contacts around the country.

So, much as I may grumble when I see new titles instituted, and much as I may sometimes resent the way the limelight of community attention is trained on contests and titleholders, I also see that they are important to the community as it is constituted today.

Given that fact, how could I counsel a person who is eager to give something back to the leather community not to seek a title? Simple. For every titleholder, and for every contestant, there are dozens or hundreds or even thousands of people who do the work of creating, supporting, and utilizing both the contest and the titleholder. From the volunteers who take tickets and pour beer at beer busts, to the donors of auction items and the entertainers in the shows; from the guys at computers who maintain mailing lists and create flyers to the ones who are constantly running errands to the copy shop or the donut shop, the opportunities to do small but vital things are endless. Every event, even one as small as a beer and soda bust to benefit a local charity, uses the talents and skills and energy of an army of volunteers. And every event could be made better, made more effective as a benefit, made more pleasurable for the community that supports it, or made more powerful as an opportunity to communicate if more people brought more skills, talents, and energy to bear on the production.

Whatever you can do, you can in some way do for the leather community. If you are a barber, donate haircuts as prizes in raffles and contests, or offer to give haircuts to PWAs who cannot go out to a barber shop. If you have an extra bedroom, offer to house visiting leatherfolk, which reduces the amount of money local events have to spend on hotels and increases the amount of money available to charities or the purposes of the event in progress. If you can sew, paint, do graphic design, or entertain, the opportunities are obvious. If you think you can do nothing, you can always do for local events and causes the things you do for yourself at home. Cooking and cleaning, reading and writing, shopping and placing phone calls are all activities anyone can do. Most people can also collect prizes or advertising commitments from local businesses or provide "taxi" service for someone who can, teach an SM technique or be a demo model for someone who can, stuff and label envelopes or provide a comfortable work space for someone who can.

People who do just about anything well often get better at it, get noticed doing it, and get involved in doing it for more events or groups and for larger events or groups. Getting involved in any way is a start; the problem then is to figure out what your own limits are, and to curtail your volunteering at a point where you are still glad to give what the community is happy to take from you.

Being a titleholder ought to be a matter of effectively representing a large number of people who will never be titleholders. When the representation is real, the whole community is given a sense of accomplishment and fulfillment by a powerful voice that speaks of and for concerns that are widely shared. Some titleholders, of course, are purely about their looks, which is fine. If we are putting hunks (mindless or not) in the position of apparent authority named by a leather title, it is because among the available options, that is the one most of us want to put into the spotlight at the time. I often find it terrifying that so many ill-prepared and inappropriate "leaders" are created instantly by title contests, but I trust the community to understand the difference between celebrity (which is each person's 15 minutes of fame) and authority (which is the effect of a well-intentioned life).

The title system, like anything that channels so much money and affects so many people, can be abused, but I think the abuses are much less common than we sometimes imagine. It works *for* most of us most of the time and, even at its worst, it gives us some spectacular opportunities to meet, play, have sex, and otherwise interact with each other.

Index

Index

Index

Index

Index

Index

Index

Index

Also available from **Daedalus Publishing Company**

www.daedaluspublishing.com

Urban Aboriginals

A Celebration of Leathersexuality

Written in its heyday in the early 1980's, author Geoff Mains explores the spiritual, sexual, emotional, cultural and physiological aspects of Leathersex. $15.95

Carried Away

An s/M Romance

In david stein's first novel, steamy leathersex is only the begining when a cocky, jaded bottom and a once-burned Master come together for some no-strings bondage and s/M. Once the scene is over, a deeper hunger unexpectedly awakens, and they begin playing for much higher stakes. $19.95

The Compleat Slave

Creating and Living an Erotic Dominant/submissive Lifestyle

In this highly anticipated follow up to *The Master's Manual*, author Jack Rinella continues his in-depth exploration of Dominant/submissive relationships. $15.95

The Master's Manual

A Handbook of Erotic Dominance

In this book, author Jack Rinella examines various aspects of erotic dominance, including S/M, safety, sex, erotic power, techniques, and more. $16.95

SlaveCraft

Roadmaps for Erotic Servitude: principles, skills and tools

Guy Baldwin, author of *Ties That Bind*, joins forces with a grateful slave to produce this gripping and personal account on the subject of consensual slavery. $15.95

Ties That Bind

The SM/Leather/Fetish Erotic Style: Issues, Commentaries and Advice

The early writings of well-known psychotherapist and respected member of the leather community Guy Baldwin have been compiled to create this SM classic. $16.95

Chainmale: 3SM

A Unique View of Leather Culture

Author Don Bastian brings his experiences to print with this fast-paced account of one man's experience with his own sexuality and eventual involvement in a loving and successful three-way kink relationship. $13.95

My Private Life

Real Experiences of a Dominant Woman

Within these pages, the author, Mistress Nan, allows the reader a brief glimpse into the true private life of an erotically dominant woman. $14.95

Leathersex

A Guide for the Curious Outsider and the Serious Player

Written by renowned S/M author Joseph Bean, the reader will find much wisdom within this volume about this often misunderstood form of erotic expression. $16.95

Consensual Sadomasochism

How to Talk About It And How to Do It Safely

Authors William A. Henkin, Ph.D., and Sybil Holiday, CCSSE, combine their knowledge and expertise in this unique examination of erotic consensual sadomasochism. $16.95

Beneath the Skins

The New Spirit and Politics of the Kink Community

This book by Ivo Dominguez, Jr., examines the many issues facing the modern leather/SM/fetish community. $12.95

Leather and Latex Care

How to Keep Your Leather and Latex Looking Great

This concise book by Kelly J. Thibault gives the reader all they need to know to keep their leather and latex items looking great. $10.95

Between the Cracks

The Daedalus Anthology of Kinky Verse

Editor Gavin Dillard has compiled this impressive selection of poetry from well-known authors that celebrates the edgier side of sexuality. $18.95

The Leather Contest Guide

A Handbook for Promoters, Contestants, Judges and Titleholders

International Mr. Leather and Mr. National Leather Association contest winner Guy Baldwin is the author of this truly complete guide to the leather contest. $12.95

Learning the Ropes

A Basic Guide to Fun S/M Lovemaking

This book by S/M expert Race Bannon guides the reader through the basics of safe and fun SM. $12.95

How to Order

By phone: 323-666-2121

By e-mail: order@DaedalusPublishing.com

By mail: Daedalus Publishing Company
2140 Hyperion Ave.
Los Angeles, CA 90027

Payment: All major credit cards are accepted. *Via e-mail or regular mail,* indicate type of card, card number, expiration date, name of cardholder as shown on card, and billing address of cardholder. Also include the mailing address where you wish your order to be sent. Orders via regular mail may include payment by money order or check, but may be held until the check clears. Make checks or money orders payable to "Daedalus Publishing Company." *Do not send cash.*

Tax and shipping: All orders, add $4.25 shipping charge for the first book and $1.00 for each additional book to the order total. California residents, add 8.25% sales tax to the total price of the books you are ordering.

Over-21 statement: Since many of our publications deal with sexuality issues, all mail orders must include a signed statement that you are at least 21 years of age. Also include such a statement with any e-mail order.